THE JOURNEY HOME

THE JOURNEY HOME

Spiritual guidance for every day

Nick Aiken

Originally published in Great Britain in 1997 as
The Journey Home: A path for pilgrim people
by Marshall Pickering, an imprint of HarperCollins*Religious*,
part of HarperCollins*Publishers*

This edition published in Great Britain in 2010

Society for Promoting Christian Knowledge
36 Causton Street
London SW1P 4ST

British Library Cataloguing-in-Publication Data
A catalogue record for this book is available from the British Library

ISBN 978-0-281-06230-0

1 3 5 7 9 10 8 6 4 2

Typeset by Graphicraft Ltd, Hong Kong
Printed in Great Britain by Ashford Colour Press

Produced on paper from sustainable forests

To Hilary, Alastair and Simon

Contents

———•◆•———

Contents

Introduction

The Journey Home consists of 40 sections which can be used at any time of the year, since our Christian journey goes on day by day throughout the year. Each section starts with a variety of biblical texts which all reflect the daily theme. A personal comment on these passages follows. Afterwards, the challenge of a practical spiritual activity to connect with the reality of our daily lives is presented. Finally, a simple prayer is offered. Each daily reading encompasses a simple truth of the Christian message, and will take you no more than five or ten minutes to read. I hope that you will dip into it, for example, while on the train commuting to work, at home over a cup of coffee or in the evening as part of your daily prayers.

I have entitled this book *The Journey Home* because that is the destination to which all of us are going. Making that journey, however, is full of distractions and discouragements, as well as joys and inspirations. *The Journey Home* offers spiritual guidance for travelling along that path, together with the more practical aspects of making a journey – the excess baggage, the essentials we need, etc.

The book may be used individually or in a group. It is designed so that each member of a group can follow the same sections for the day, reflect on the questions provided which draw upon the passages and discuss and share their thoughts on the message contained therein.

My hope and prayer is that all of us will find much encouragement from the inspiring and powerful message that comes to us from the Bible to help us on our journey home.

Nick Aiken
Pyrford, Woking

1

Where are we going?

THE FIRST DAY

Leaving the old securities

Bible readings

The Lord had said to Abram, 'Leave your country, your people and your father's household and go to the land I will show you. I will make you into a great nation and I will bless you; I will make your name great, and you will be a blessing. I will bless those who bless you, and whoever curses you I will curse; and all peoples on earth will be blessed through you.' So Abram left, as the Lord had told him; and Lot went with him.

(Genesis 12.1–4)

Now a man came up to Jesus and asked, 'Teacher, what good thing must I do to get eternal life?' 'Why do you ask me about what is good?' Jesus replied. 'There is only One who is good. If you want to enter life, obey the commandments.' 'Which ones?' the man enquired. Jesus replied, 'Do not murder, do not commit adultery, do not steal, do not give false testimony, honour your father and mother and love your neighbour as yourself.' 'All these I have kept,' the young man said. 'What do I still lack?'

Jesus answered, 'If you want to be perfect, go, sell your possessions and give to the poor, and you will have treasure in heaven. Then come, follow me.'

(Matthew 19.16–21)

* * *

1

Letting go – leaving the warmth and security of what we know – defeats many of us a lot of the time. We generally like to live ordered, certain lives, and to be clear about what we can rely on. Little wonder, then, that moving house or leaving home can be stressful experiences. You were settled in your home; everything had its place and could be found. You stamped your own personality on your house or room, and it reflected your own emotions and preferences. Now that has changed; all that you rely on, in terms of knowing where things are, is thrown into confusion. You have left part of yourself behind in the place where you have come from. This all culminates in stress, because you have had to let go, move forward and begin life in a new way and in a different location.

As Christians, our spiritual life challenges us to move on and change. We are called to leave behind our human securities and respond to the call of God. That is the frightening, yet exciting, dynamic of faith. Over the next few weeks we are going to make a journey, a pilgrimage. We are going to look at ourselves and at God. Hopefully, by looking at God, we will be led into a deeper knowledge and understanding of who he is, and who we are as children called by him. You have got to be prepared, however, to encounter and accept the rigours of that journey. You will have to let go and leave behind. You will even need to turn your back on certain aspects of your life – those old securities which are comfortable and attractive, but of no value.

Abram was called by God to let go and leave behind, and I am sure he was frightened by the prospect. He was asked to give up what was most dear to him – his family, his friends and his country. He was called to make a sacrifice and take a risk. The question remained, was that risk worth taking? Likewise, the rich young man had to look at the risk of forfeiting the security of what he had built up. He probably was used to taking risks in accumulating his wealth and speculated when necessary. But when it came to the biggest risk of his life – following Jesus – he could not cope. We never find out what finally happened to him. From the Bible's point of view, there is no more story to be told; he disappears because he rules himself out of God's plan and purpose for his life.

We *do* know what happened to Abram. His story was told because he did leave behind the old securities, and he followed the call of God. His life became infinitely more creative, dynamic and of greater significance because he went on that journey of faith. He went with God. That is what we are called to do: to forget about the shallow attractions of our engineered, developed, personal securities which mean so much to us, but which can be easily overturned by the unpredictable changes over which we have no control. We may be so busy expending a great deal of effort creating external certainties which help to give our life meaning, that we fail to recognize that, at the heart of it, we *ourselves* need to change. We need to become more like Christ, to be made in his image, and to have the strength that comes from knowing him, and following his call on our lives. The rest of it does not really matter. I agree with that well-known phrase: 'Let go and let God'.

Spiritual activity

Pause for a moment and look at your life and your present relationship with God. List the personal securities which are important to you, and then reflect on whether they or any aspect of them hinder your trust in God. Then decide what you are going to do about them. Allow God's Spirit and your God-given conscience to speak to you and illuminate the spiritual reality of what you need to leave behind.

Prayer

Lord, help me to let go. Help me to leave behind all the securities which hinder a deeper faith and trust in you. Give me courage to hold your hand and take the risk of following your will for my life. Amen.

THE SECOND DAY

The spiritual realities: compassion

Bible readings

So Moses chiselled out two stone tablets like the first ones and went up Mount Sinai early in the morning, as the Lord had commanded him; and he carried the two stone tablets in his hands. Then the Lord came down in the cloud and stood there with him and proclaimed his name, 'the Lord'. And he passed in front of Moses, proclaiming, 'The Lord, the Lord, the compassionate and gracious God, slow to anger, abounding in love and faithfulness, maintaining love to thousands, and forgiving wickedness, rebellion and sin. Yet he does not leave the guilty unpunished; he punishes the children and their children for the sin of the fathers to the third and fourth generation.'

(Exodus 34.4–7)

For the Lord will vindicate his people
and have compassion on his servants.

(Psalm 135.14)

Jesus had compassion on them and touched their eyes. Immediately they received their sight and followed him.

(Matthew 20.34)

* * *

On a spiritual journey you will never receive a full picture or understanding of where it is that you are going; you can only glimpse the reality of the destination that lies before you. The exciting dimension about the Christian faith, however, is that we are called to know the one who is leading us to that final destination. We are called to turn our back on the things that have no substance or reality, and trust in the one who is true and never changes – God himself. Yet who is this God? What does he reveal of himself that encourages us to trust him for the future? If we are going to make this spiritual journey we

4

must be clear about the point at which we are starting: the nature and person of God as he reveals himself to us.

Right from the beginning, when God gave the Law to Moses, he reveals himself as a God of compassion. A compassionate person is someone who sees, understands and then comes alongside you. For example, someone who is there for you when your baby dies, or when your marriage fails; when you are told you no longer have a job, and you stand on the verge of a nervous breakdown; when you fail your exams; when you are ill; or when you are in trouble and upset. A compassionate person is someone who stands with you when a longed-for success becomes a reality, and the dreams for which you toiled and sweated so hard finally come true.

God is a God of compassion; he has a heart which sees and understands. He sees the way you are feeling and the fullness of the circumstances that you are in. How is he able to show such compassion? Because he knows. He knows you and he knows all about you. It is only those friends and family who know us well who can say, 'What is wrong?' They can see if we are troubled or disturbed without us uttering a word. It is a sense, a mood or a glance that tells it all. Cherish your friends who are compassionate and hold on to them, because they have your real interests and concerns at heart. God is just like this – his feeling for you is genuine. He is not trying to manipulate you; he does not want to obtain something from you in return. He sees, he understands and he comes alongside.

Yet, often we think God is there to disapprove and condemn. It may be our guilt that is screaming at us, but do not confuse this guilt with God. Such is his compassion that he sees the mess and muddle that we get into, understands why we have ended up there, and still comes to help us out. If we had consulted him in the first place there would not be such a mess. But he does not hold the fact that we wanted to do it our way against us; he responds when we genuinely turn to him. Even when we are victims of forces and people who have control over our lives, he promises to vindicate his servants. Why? Because of his nature and character.

If we are going to make this journey we have got to be clear about who it is we trust – God – and focus our eyes on him. Do not embark on the journey without a knowledge of the realities of the nature of God, because you will not have the resources to continue.

Spiritual activity

Think of your friends who show compassion to you and your family.

- What recent gesture and action displayed that compassion?
- What did this mean to you?

Prayer

Lord, I appreciate you and who you are. I see in you a depth and beauty that speaks of genuine compassion. Help me to sense the reality of the way you see and respond to my life in all its complexities. Help me to understand as I am understood by you. Amen.

THE THIRD DAY

The spiritual realities: grace

Bible readings

The Word became flesh and made his dwelling among us. We have seen his glory, the glory of the One and Only, who came from the Father, full of grace and truth. John testifies concerning him. He cries out, saying, 'This was he of whom I said, "He who comes after me has surpassed me because he was before me."' From the fullness of his grace we have all received one blessing after another. For the law was given through Moses; grace and truth through Jesus Christ.

(John 1.14–17)

For all have sinned and fall short of the glory of God, and are justified freely by his grace through the redemption that came by Christ Jesus.

(Romans 3.23–24)

In him we have redemption through his blood, the forgiveness of sins, in accordance with the riches of God's grace that he lavished on us with all wisdom and understanding. And he made known to us the mystery of his will according to his good pleasure, which he purposed in Christ, to be put into effect when the times will have reached their fulfilment – to bring all things in heaven and on earth together under one head, even Christ.

(Ephesians 1.7–10)

* * *

Grace is a word that hardly comes into common usage. You will not find it in the daily newspaper or use it in conversation with your friends. Grace, for many years, was a hidden word; I personally had no real concept of its significance or meaning. To know what a word means you have to identify something with it. You know what the word 'chair' means, because everyone knows the object that is associated with it. When a word is linked with something which is not physically tangible, however, all of us can struggle with its true meaning.

It was not a theological degree that taught me the definition of the word 'grace', it was an experience of the living God. Only when you experience the grace of God can you begin to understand the word's meaning. Grace means the free and unconditional love of God, or the enjoyment of God's favour. Many of you might be under the illusion that you need to earn God's love and that you do this by being good. You might believe that the relationship is conditional: you behave and do good deeds, and God will approve and be favourable to you. This is heresy. The truth is that God has fallen in love with you. It is when we realize this spiritual reality that we are liberated into the freedom of faith. We can never be good enough; our love and faith will always be inadequate and we will always be aware of their weakness. But we are not dependent on what we offer to God. He is unconditional love, and as an act of grace, he offers to us his friendship and love.

This is the exciting dynamic of faith; the process of falling in love always enables you to discover and experience a greater depth of faith and reality. It is a journey that has no end. The Scriptures speak about the lavishness of God's grace. 'Lavishness' tends to be a word which is associated with a self-indulgent, materialistic spoiling of oneself. But it has a very different meaning when understood as an action expressed to someone else, as a gesture of love. With God we are the recipients of that gesture.

He gives, he shares, he embraces and he lavishes his love on us because we mean so much to him. We are his creation; as great as is the creative force that he has let loose in the making of the cosmos, so also is the power of his very nature of grace and love. As we wonder at the creation of the world around us, so we can wonder at the free, unmerited grace that he shows to us in Christ.

Expressing love for someone is a risky business. It changes the nature of a friendship. One party of the relationship can either sustain such a declaration of feeling and reciprocate it, or may not feel the same way – unable to accept what is being offered – and break up the relationship. So it is with God. He has taken the risk of expressing his unmerited love to us as an act of grace. Either we accept, respond and begin the exciting journey of discovery that that entails, or we shy away, never to discover what an intoxicating and powerful relationship could have taken place.

Spiritual activity

Think of someone whom you love and cherish. Then, consider what would be an appropriate, lavish gesture which expresses your feelings for him or her, and respects his or her own individuality. When you have considered what to do, carry it out. When it is complete, ask yourself what this has told you about God and your relationship with him.

Prayer

Father, I do not fully understand or comprehend the magnitude of your love. Yet in Christ I see your love being freely offered. Teach me to perceive the reality of your grace. Help me to know the truth of your favour, and help me to discover the depths of the power of your love. I ask this for Christ's sake. Amen.

THE FOURTH DAY

The spiritual realities: abounding in love...

Bible readings

But you, O Lord, are a compassionate and gracious God, slow to anger, abounding in love and faithfulness.

(Psalm 86.15)

Who shall separate us from the love of Christ? Shall trouble or hardship or persecution or famine or nakedness or danger or sword? As it is written: 'For your sake we face death all day long; we are considered as sheep to be slaughtered.' No, in all these things we are more than conquerors through him who loved us. For I am convinced that neither death nor life, neither angels nor demons, neither the present nor the future, nor any powers, neither height nor depth nor anything else in all creation, will be able to separate us from the love of God that is in Christ Jesus our Lord.

(Romans 8.35–39)

But when the kindness and love of God our Saviour appeared, he saved us, not because of righteous things we had done, but because of his mercy. He saved us through the washing of rebirth and renewal of the Holy Spirit, whom he poured out on us generously through Jesus Christ our Saviour, so that, having been justified by his grace, we might become heirs having the hope of eternal life.

(Titus 3.4–7)

* * *

According to *The Oxford Illustrated Dictionary*, to abound means to be plentiful, indeed, to be rich in. Therefore, to describe God as abounding in love is a wonderful way of expressing that his love is plentiful because he is so rich in love. God has so much love that he does not have to ration it out or divide it up so that everyone gets a small amount. He is abounding in love, he is rich in it; he can give it to everyone freely and without measure. But this giving does not end there. God does not give away his love to us, only for us simply to walk away and do whatever we want. His love is so strong and powerful that we cannot go beyond the point of its source and influence. The shattering truth is that no human or cosmic experience can separate us from the reality of the love that God has for us. There is no force in creation that is stronger or more powerful that it can divide us from that love. We think of the awesome strength of a thermonuclear weapon, which in itself pales into insignificance compared with the forces of nature, and yet God's love is even more powerful. Little wonder St Paul realized the spiritual reality as he walked with God and exclaimed, 'For I am convinced...'!

If ever you become doubtful that God loves you, just look at the Cross. Look, do not just glance! Instead of making it a passing thought or a vague reference, stare, gaze and consider that he caused his Son to be crucified on the Cross out of love for you. At times, when life seems to be going anywhere but our way, and we are surrounded by tragedy and failure, we need to keep our eyes firmly fixed on the Cross and the spiritual reality of God's love. It is at these times that we may question where are we going and where are we being led, but we must remember that we go with God. He is the one who travels alongside us; he abounds in love. What a great travelling companion!

I have frequently questioned and argued with God about the direction of my life. The course of events and circumstances sometimes seemed too painful and too difficult to follow. I have often felt like a frontline soldier who is at the receiving end of direct combat. Battle fatigued and occasionally shellshocked I would wonder, 'Why me?'; 'Why do I have to be vulnerable and at the rough end of life – all alone?' I would shout at God and ask him to make things easier, to change the circumstances, because I could see no purpose in the direction in which I was being taken.

God *did* hear my prayers, he did not let me down; I think now that I can begin to see the reason why. I do not want to go down that road again, but I probably will. The Christian journey calls us to take up our own cross and follow Christ, and that hurts – really hurts – at times. We may not understand what befalls us in our life, and the circumstances we find ourselves in, but what we are called to understand is the abundant love God has for us; and we find that supremely shown in the Cross of Christ.

Spiritual activity

During the day, make the effort to take time out to be alone. Focus your thoughts and imagination on the Cross. Spend some time looking at the scene: the blood and sweat on Christ's body; the pain and anguish on his face; the pierced hands and feet; the large and coarse nails. Imagine yourself as one of the crowd. Stay focused on the scene for as long as is appropriate, and when you have finished simply say, 'Thank you'.

Prayer

Thanks be to thee, my Lord Jesus Christ, for all the benefits which you have won for me, for all the pains and insults which you have borne for me. O most merciful Redeemer, Friend and Brother, may I know you more clearly, love you more dearly, and follow you more nearly, day by day. Amen.

(St Richard of Chichester)

THE FIFTH DAY

The spiritual realities:... and faithfulness

Bible readings

I will sing of the Lord's great love for ever;
with my mouth I will make your faithfulness known
through all generations.
I will declare that your love stands firm for ever,
that you established your faithfulness in heaven itself.

(Psalm 89.1–2)

The Lord did not set his affection on you and choose you because you were more numerous than other peoples, for you were the fewest of all peoples. But it was because the Lord loved you and kept the oath he swore to your forefathers that he brought you out with a mighty hand and redeemed you from the land of slavery, from the power of Pharaoh king of Egypt. Know therefore that the Lord your God is God; he is the faithful God, keeping his covenant of love to a thousand generations of those who love him and keep his commands.

(Deuteronomy 7.7–9)

Therefore, brothers, since we have confidence to enter the Most Holy Place by the blood of Jesus, by a new and living way opened for us through the curtain, that is, his body, and since we have a great priest over the house of God, let us draw near to God with a sincere heart in full assurance of faith, having our hearts sprinkled to cleanse us from a guilty conscience and having our bodies washed with pure water. Let us hold unswervingly to the hope we profess, for he who promised is faithful.

(Hebrews 10.19–23)

* * *

Whatever our political views, there are some individuals who gain our admiration because of the extent they are prepared to suffer for what they believe in. I do not mean those who advocate any form of violence to promote their cause; rather, those who – for the cause of social and political justice – suffer prolonged prison sentences at the hands of repressive regimes. There are those who are world-renowned figures and who have large-scale campaigns to secure their release.

Tragically, there are many more unknown individuals who suffer merely for what they believe to be right. They do not have any public recognition to sustain them, or the benefit of the influence of foreign governments with their threats of economic penalties. These people suffer alone in the cause of justice. The only hope that sustains them is their desire to be faithful to what they believe to be true. In the twentieth century alone, more Christians suffered for their faith and paid the ultimate price of martyrdom than at any time since the dawn of the Christian Church. Whether it was at the hands of the Communist political commissars, or Idi Amin's reign of terror in Uganda, or in the Nazi death camps, untold men and women have kept faith with the one who is faithful to us. And for that they have paid the greatest price.

Throughout the Bible we discover that part of the very nature of God is his faithfulness, and that this faithfulness is not conditional but constant. The political and religious history of the children of Israel tells of a people who wander away from God and who are faithless in the face of God's care for them. However, God constantly calls them back to himself. He does not give up on them, or wash his hands of them in the light of their disobedience. Despite their spiritual adultery he is faithful. He had rescued them from Egypt, and by signs and great wonders delivered them to the promised land. Yet so often they compromised their beliefs and found other gods to worship, rather like our own generation. They must have broken God's heart. But he would not let go because he was faithful to those he loved. Moreover, he kept that faith by sending Christ – his ultimate act of faithfulness – to a lost and broken world.

We may not be challenged to display the same faithfulness to a cause that some individuals in our generation are asked to do. However, as we make our way through life we need to grasp the reality that God is faithful to us out of his own choice. Despite the disappointment we may cause him and the lack of commitment that we may exhibit, he does not turn his back on us; he is persistent and holds on to us. In fact, we are encouraged to come closer to God, not confident in our own goodness and our own qualifications, but rather in the knowledge that he has paid the entry price into his presence for us. The way is always open. God is the ultimate faithful partner.

Spiritual activity

At some stage during the day, jot down the names of any famous people who are faithful to their cause. Then add to that list any people known personally to you who are faithful in their relationships, despite difficult circumstances. What qualities do they possess that you admire?

Prayer

O faithful Father, help me to stay close to you. Help me not to ignore your advice and commands. Help me to be faithful to you and your Word, especially when the easy option would be to compromise and take the convenient path. I pray this in the name of my Saviour, Jesus Christ. Amen.

THE SIXTH DAY

The spiritual realities: forgiveness and justice

Bible readings

If my people, who are called by my name, will humble themselves and pray and seek my face and turn from their wicked ways, then will I hear from heaven and will forgive their sin and will heal their land.

(2 Chronicles 7.14)

The Lord our God is merciful and forgiving, even though we have rebelled against him.

(Daniel 9.9)

If we claim to be without sin, we deceive ourselves and the truth is not in us. If we confess our sins, he is faithful and just and will forgive us our sins and purify us from all unrighteousness.

(1 John 1.8–9)

If his sons forsake my law and do not follow my statutes,
if they violate my decrees and fail to keep my commands,
I will punish their sin with the rod, their iniquity with flogging;
but I will not take my love from him, nor will I ever betray my
  faithfulness.

(Psalm 89.30–33)

* * *

As we come to the end of this first section we have asked the question, 'Where are we going?' The answer, of course, is we do not know. How could we possibly know? We are not party to that sort of knowledge and understanding. The critical knowledge to possess concerns the realities that we take with us along our journey of faith, and we will be developing this issue later. So far we have endeavoured to look at the essential nature of the one who we are called to follow and obey. We

16

now turn to the final aspect of God that we will be considering – forgiveness and justice.

Sadly, many of us think that to forgive someone means to dispense with justice; if a person has done something wrong he or she needs to be punished. Because God is a God of forgiveness, it does not mean he forgets about punishment and the exercise of the appropriate judgement. For a Christian to say that he or she does not believe in hell, and that a loving God could not possibly condemn someone to hell, is to distort the concept of justice. If there is no hell then presumably Adolf Hitler shares the same fate as Mother Teresa. For that to be true it makes a mockery of any sense of right and wrong.

God's essential nature, however, is to forgive. He not only offers it to us if we request it, but also provides the means by which that forgiveness can be obtained. God is more ready to forgive us than we are to forgive ourselves. We may wish to punish ourselves for what we have done wrong, and feel we need to torture ourselves with a sense of unremitting remorse before accepting that we have paid the price for our actions. But the reality of God's forgiveness breaks upon us like the beauty of a sunlit dawn. It can be seen by everyone; although each of us has defied God and gone our own way in life, he still offers reconciliation and forgiveness when we turn to him and say we are sorry. He does not produce a logbook of wrongdoing and demand a full explanation accompanied by the requisite punishment. Rather, if our confession is genuine and we do desire to follow God's direction for our lives, he offers forgiveness to us; and the person who has offered to take the responsibility of accepting the punishment is Christ himself.

Christ accepts the judgement because our sin has to be dealt with and accounted for. It is Jesus who accepts that responsibility and as a result justice prevails. On the Cross he accepted the price and condemnation for our sin so that we could walk free. It is to Christ that we owe our debt of gratitude.

Spiritual activity

- Is there anyone who comes to mind who has recently forgiven you for something you have done wrong? (It may have been your spouse, parents, a neighbour or work colleague.)
- What did their act of forgiveness make you feel?
- Are there any lessons you can learn about God's forgiveness from that action?

Prayer

Father, when I most needed forgiveness you were there offering it to me. There was nothing I could do but say I was sorry. I saw that it was Christ who came and took the blame for all that I did and yet I continue to do wrong. Help me to always seek your will and way for my life. Amen.

2

Excess baggage

———•◦•———

THE SEVENTH DAY

The tears of pain

Bible readings

Now one of the Pharisees invited Jesus to have dinner with him, so he went to the Pharisee's house and reclined at the table. When a woman who had lived a sinful life in that town learned that Jesus was eating at the Pharisee's house, she brought an alabaster jar of perfume, and as she stood behind him at his feet weeping, she began to wet his feet with her tears. Then she wiped them with her hair, kissed them and poured perfume on them.

(Luke 7.36–38)

When the Lord brought back the captives to Zion,
we were like men who dreamed.
Our mouths were filled with laughter,
our tongues with songs of joy.
Then it was said among the nations,
'The Lord has done great things for them.'
The Lord has done great things for us, and we are filled with
    joy.
Restore our fortunes, O Lord, like streams in the Negev.
Those who sow in tears will reap with songs of joy.
He who goes out weeping, carrying seed to sow,
will return with songs of joy, carrying sheaves with him.

(Psalm 126)

'Therefore, they are before the throne of God and serve him day and night in his temple; and he who sits on the throne will spread his tent over them. Never again will they hunger; never again will they thirst. The sun will not beat upon them, nor any scorching heat. For the Lamb at the centre of the throne will be their shepherd; he will lead them to springs of living water. And God will wipe away every tear from their eyes.'

(Revelation 7.15–17)

* * *

A person who has never cried is a person who does not know himself or herself, and does not truly know God. Tears are very beautiful because they express what we genuinely feel, they are an honest expression of our emotions. This is certainly true of the moving story of the woman in Luke's Gospel, who wipes Jesus' feet with her ointment and her tears. It is a touching episode because she had only known and given a love that was confused and probably abused by others. The love she experienced was essentially physical and superficial, and yet when she came to Christ he put her in touch with her true, inner feelings, and the result was many tears being shed.

This woman, however, is no different to many of us who, when we come to Jesus and acknowledge his pure love for us, recognize all that spoils and disappoints us in our lives and are moved to tears – tears of pain for the past and tears of repentance. We have to acknowledge all the excess baggage in our lives that we have carried around with us for far too long, and confess and give it to God. To hold on to it will only impede our journey; it will stunt our spiritual growth.

A real meeting and walk with Christ gets right to the heart of our lives. He reaches the depths of our being and longing because we cannot hide anything from him. It is true for all of us, no matter how long we have been believers. At times, we can keep God at a distance but it is only when we truly turn to him again in a fresh, new and honest way that we are profoundly aware of who we genuinely are, and what we feel about our lives. When we are in touch with these honest feelings, then the reaction can produce tears – tears which are expressive of all that we feel, all that we know about ourselves and all that we are sorry for.

The current thinking that 'real men do not cry' is so pathetically inadequate that it is nothing more than vain conceit. The woman who encountered Jesus did not cry simply because she was a woman; she cried because she knew herself, and she knew the one whose feet she wept over and anointed. God's love for us does not discriminate between the sexes; it reaches out to everyone. For the woman in the story, the impure love she had experienced met the pure love of God and, as a result, she realized all the pain and ugliness that had gone on before.

On several occasions, we will be brought to tears along the path of our journey with God, because it is then that we will see the real worth of those areas of our lives which we may not have wanted to acknowledge or evaluate. Yet, despite the pain and grief we may suffer on these occasions, they are marks of our spiritual progress and inner healing. They represent an inner cleansing from the pride, the arrogance, the resentment and the disobedience that festers above and below the surface of our lives.

Spiritual activity

Think back to the last time when you were moved to tears by something you encountered. It may have been something that affected you or, indeed, someone else you were aware of. Then ask yourself the question, 'What areas of my life cause me such pain and regret that at times they evoke tears?' Reflect on these matters and tell God what you genuinely feel about them, as well as your hopes and fears as to how these situations may work out.

Prayer

Lord, there is no area of my life that is hidden from you.
Yet, often I hold on to what I want to possess or do. I prefer to
go my own way and only hurt you and myself in the process.
Shine the light of your integrity and love into my whole being
so that I have only an open and honest relationship with you.
Amen.

THE EIGHTH DAY

The regrets

Bible readings

Therefore, since we are surrounded by such a great cloud of witnesses, let us throw off everything that hinders and the sin that so easily entangles, and let us run with perseverance the race marked out for us. Let us fix our eyes on Jesus, the author and perfecter of our faith, who for the joy set before him endured the cross, scorning its shame, and sat down at the right hand of the throne of God.

(Hebrews 12.1–2)

Therefore, if anyone is in Christ, he is a new creation; the old has gone, the new has come! All this is from God, who reconciled us to himself through Christ and gave us the ministry of reconciliation: that God was reconciling the world to himself in Christ, not counting men's sins against them. And he has committed to us the message of reconciliation.

(2 Corinthians 5.17–19)

Jesus replied, 'No-one who puts his hand to the plough and looks back is fit for service in the kingdom of God.'

(Luke 9.62)

* * *

Most people have a favourite sport; while they may not necessarily play it themselves, they may well be enthusiastic supporters and avid viewers when it is on the television. With individual track events the particular word which seems to have been very much in vogue in recent years is 'focus'. The word is really used to describe a body, mind and spirit concentration on the task in hand. Your whole being is directed to achieving the goal before you. In this situation there are very strong parallels with our Christian faith: we are called to fix our eyes on Jesus; he is to be our focus as we journey along the path of faith.

23

Invariably, however, we carry with us the baggage of regrets and guilt about the past. Let us be honest, these regrets can understandably be very real: for example, we did not want our marriage to break up – when we took our vows we never for one moment envisaged that the relationship would end in the way that it did; we never wanted there to be such a difficult relationship with our son or daughter or parents. We all have hopes and aspirations about aspects of our lives; when they fail to materialize the regret can be very difficult to live with. Not only may we have regrets about personal relationships but also about ourselves, how we handled matters and what we did wrong. We may be paying the price for weeks, months, years – even a lifetime – for what we have done. That can be painful and hard to live with. There can be very few people in life who do not look back and wish they had dealt with a certain situation and relationship in a different way. Usually, those with no regrets about anything have no real sensitivity or deep love for others, and are hijacked by their own conceit.

Since regrets can be such a crippling expression of what we feel about ourselves and others, it is crucial to let the spiritual message breathe into our lives and bring healing and reconciliation. We must not let the past and the sadness of disappointed hopes, for example, deflect us and hamper our growth for the future. We should focus on Jesus who knows, understands and forgives us. Furthermore, when we turn over our lives to Christ, such is the power and significance of this act's implications that the Scriptures say we are a new person. The old person has died with the past and a new person has emerged. All the regrettable and ugly things that shaped our lives before we came to Christ are now superseded by our new purpose and direction, as we let our lives be guided by God.

Even as Christians we make mistakes and become deflected from what we should do, but the way of forgiveness and reconciliation is always open and available. The past need not haunt us or overshadow us. We can learn from our mistakes and leave our regrets behind. Sometimes we can even learn to avoid later regrets, by recognizing those actions which, though attractive at the time, will compromise our spiritual values. When I got engaged to the woman who is now my wife, it would have been easy to have had sexual intercourse. We both longed for that close expression of love. The only constraint that stopped us was our Christian understanding of marriage, and the place of sex within it. But we also recognized that for many years we had individually kept to those beliefs, and that to fall at the final hurdle would only cause a deep sense of regret and failure. So we waited until our wedding night, and I am so glad we did.

Jesus encourages and challenges us not to look back and get caught up in the distractions that hinder our spiritual growth. It is harmful to keep dwelling on what you cannot change and is in the past. It is over and done with, so give it to God. The words of a well-known hymn come to mind: 'I have decided to follow Jesus, no turning back, no turning back.' Good advice.

Spiritual activity

Scribble on a piece of paper the areas of your life and relationships which cause you a sense of regret. Then reflect on how you can be reconciled to those people and those situations. Put the piece of paper in your Bible, and when you have done all in your power to resolve these situations, tear up the piece of paper and do not look back.

Prayer

Lord, I cannot undo the past. I can only be reconciled to it and leave it behind. Help me to move forward, looking to you as the focus and source of my faith. Amen.

THE NINTH DAY

The failures

Bible readings

'Will the Lord reject for ever? Will he never show his favour again?

Has his unfailing love vanished for ever? Has his promise failed for all time?

Has God forgotten to be merciful? Has he in anger withheld his compassion?'

Then I thought, 'To this I will appeal: the years of the right hand of the Most High.'

I will remember the deeds of the Lord; yes, I will remember your miracles of long ago.

I will meditate on all your works and consider all your mighty deeds.

Your ways, O God, are holy. What god is so great as our God?

(Psalm 77.7–13)

Therefore, since we have a great high priest who has gone through the heavens, Jesus the Son of God, let us hold firmly to the faith we profess. For we do not have a high priest who is unable to sympathize with our weaknesses, but we have one who has been tempted in every way, just as we are – yet was without sin. Let us then approach the throne of grace with confidence, so that we may receive mercy and find grace to help us in our time of need.

(Hebrews 4.14–16)

To him who is able to keep you from falling and to present you before his glorious presence without fault and with great joy – to the only God our Saviour be glory, majesty, power and authority, through Jesus Christ our Lord, before all ages, now and for evermore! Amen.

(Jude 24–25)

* * *

Sometimes we can be a prisoner to our own failure. While in some instances the fault may be entirely our own, in others it may be due to circumstances completely beyond our control. It may be the failure to be a good mother or father, or the failure to be understanding or patient which spoils our most important relationships. It is far easier to feel a success in life in terms of having the correct material possessions. But our most difficult achievement is to be a successful person. Many of the great figures of history accomplished a great deal from a military, political or economic perspective, but as individuals their lives were a mess. They were not at peace with themselves or with their families. Despite being noted for their achievements in other fields, as individuals they showed the same human frailties as the rest of us. In fact, sometimes they had more to learn than most.

The Christian faith challenges us to look at ourselves and to see ourselves as God sees us. What we earn, the kind of house we live in, and what we drive are ultimately not of importance to him. What *is* significant is the person we are: our values and priorities, our personal lifestyle and the way we treat other people. This is often where we fail. As a Christian leader, I often hear people making the comment that although they do not go to church they are intrinsically good. But, of course, by whose judgement are they good people? Is it God's perspective or, more conveniently, their own? The answer is invariably the latter. On the spiritual path of life we are asked to measure ourselves against the perfect example of Christ, because he is the model of a truly successful human. It was never God's purpose, though, to set us an impossible task or a goal that could never be obtained. Rather, he aims to point us in the right direction and ensure we do not fall into the trap of human self-righteousness.

If, however, we compare ourselves to Christ then we have failed; we will continue to do so every day, trapped by our own temperament and shortcomings, our bad moods and irritability.

Our sense of failure can embrace and cover so much of our lives because it is personal to us and the way we feel about ourselves, as well as being tied in to the regard others have for us. On this point, the Psalmist gives incredibly sound advice: do not rely on what you feel; you may feel a failure and that God has rejected you, but focus on what he has done; God is to be found in his actions and deeds and supremely in Christ; it is Christ who sympathizes with us, he is the one who is able to keep us from falling; he also goes further – he actually presents us before God; he is not ashamed of us, does not regard us as failures, and does not condemn, but understands and is there to help.

Spiritual activity

Ask yourself the question, 'What is it in my life that disappoints me and makes me feel a failure?' Having thought about it for a few moments, tell God all that you feel about these areas, and ask him to give you his perspective on your life.

Prayer

Lord, sometimes I feel a failure; I feel accused by the things that seem to defeat me. Help me to see the value of my life from your viewpoint, and help me to forgive myself as you forgive me. Amen.

THE TENTH DAY

The emptiness

Bible readings

Nebuchadnezzar, king of Babylon, has devoured us, he has thrown us into confusion, he has made us an empty jar. Like a serpent he has swallowed us and filled his stomach with our delicacies, and then has spewed us out.

(Jeremiah 51.34)

Now I am going to him who sent me, yet none of you asks me, 'Where are you going?'. Because I have said these things, you are filled with grief. But I tell you the truth: it is for your good that I am going away. Unless I go away, the Counsellor will not come to you; but if I go, I will send him to you.

(John 16.5–7)

May the God of hope fill you with all joy and peace as you trust in him, so that you may overflow with hope by the power of the Holy Spirit.

(Romans 15.13)

* * *

The link between the passages from Jeremiah and John does not at first seem obvious, but there is a profound similarity – they both touch on people's feelings of insecurity. The children of Israel had fallen victim to the ascendant power of the Babylonian empire under Nebuchadnezzar. They were exiled in a foreign land and felt devastated and empty. Life seemed hopeless. All that was familiar had gone. Their personal and corporate human resources failed them because they had none left. There was nothing more that they could call upon.

Likewise, the disciples were thrown into a state of insecurity when the one that they had followed for three years announced that he was leaving. They, too, were devastated. What were they to do? They had put their trust and confidence in Jesus and they could not live without him. The thought of his departure filled them with grief, record the Gospels.

It is good to give of yourself, but when you have got nothing left to give you are left staring into the emptiness of your own spirit and that can create a deep sense of despair. It may be that we find ourselves caught in circumstances like the children of Israel, in which we are the victims and over which we seem to have no control. Perhaps the one we love is no longer with us; maybe we have lost a job or a house. All the securities that we once knew have gone and we just feel empty and alone. This is an experience that most of us have felt at one time or another, and depending on how painful it was, we still carry the marks of those feelings with us.

I have prayed for almost a decade for someone I love dearly. I am very close to that person for all sorts of reasons, but partly because he has shared the same situation and circumstances as me. We have experienced the same emptiness, but my circumstances have changed, his have not. It causes me a real sense of pain to think of that person, and part of me feels unable to pray for him continually because I feel I have done all I can. We can feel very empty inside because that is what we feel about ourselves, or because, faced with other people's pain and sorrow, we just do not know what to say or do. We feel totally inadequate.

However, there is one experience that can be guaranteed as part of life – that there will always be change. Nothing ever stays the same, and that is part of the hope that God gives to us. There is a time for tears and a time for laughter; a time for sorrow and a time for joy. To have experienced that emptiness where God seems to have been so silent, actually gives you a gift. That gift is empathy: the ability to know and understand what others feel. If you use that gift it can be a tremendous source of encouragement to others. However, if you let that emptiness stand isolated and unreconciled in the past, it will weigh down your Christian journey and become excess baggage.

Spiritual activity

- What have been the low points in your life?
- How have you used those experiences to help others?

Prayer

Lord, it is so difficult to live with your silence when there seems to be no way out of the emptiness. Please come to me afresh and renew my spirit. Amen.

THE ELEVENTH DAY

Honest with ourselves

Bible readings

If we claim to be without sin, we deceive ourselves and the truth is not in us. If we confess our sins, he is faithful and just and will forgive us our sins and purify us from all unrighteousness. If we claim we have not sinned, we make him out to be a liar and his word has no place in our lives.

(1 John 1.8–10)

Such confidence as this is ours through Christ before God. Not that we are competent to claim anything for ourselves, but our competence comes from God.

(2 Corinthians 3.4–5)

* * *

Looking in a mirror is something we all do, usually first thing in the morning and last thing at night. When we look at ourselves we often wish that we could change certain features. For example, our nose is not the right shape; our skin pigment is not perfect; our hair is going grey or beginning to recede. Unless we are prepared to pay for very expensive cosmetic surgery, we have to live with the face that nature has given us.

The mirror reflects an honest and true picture. What it does not do is give us an emotional, psychological or spiritual reflection of ourselves. Getting a balanced and informed view of that perspective is a much more difficult process. As I have previously mentioned, people often say to me that they are good, that they live a good life. But they usually say that to justify themselves on some matter; at the heart of it, they judge themselves to be good from their own perspective. It is interesting to note that Jesus did not judge *himself* to be good, but said 'There is only One who is good' (Matthew 19.17) – in other

32

words, the Father. Jesus would not make a value judgement about himself from his own individual view; rather, he left that in the hands of God. After all, in the end it is God who is the final judge. Those who reckon themselves to be good from their own perspective might be in for a shock on the Day of Judgement, because they do not hold the scales of spiritual and personal judgement.

In order to be honest with ourselves and to get to the heart of spiritual reality, we must see ourselves and our lives from God's perspective. To do anything else is to participate in deceit. It is no good pretending that every aspect of our lives is consistent with the will of God, when we make that judgement from our own viewpoint. If our views regarding others, our business ethics, our sexual behaviour, our personal habits, our value systems and our priorities are exclusively reserved for our own judgement and not God's, then who are we deceiving?

A less-than-honest understanding of our past and previous actions can debilitate our whole spiritual progress, and act as excess baggage that impedes our growth. True honesty needs to be applied to every area of our lives. We need to observe ourselves from the perspective of the one who can give a clear and dispassionate judgement, who knows us for what we are, and who alone is the arbiter of what is of real value and worth. In this life, we as individuals will never fully understand ourselves, so complete knowledge is not acquired in any absolute sense. But we *can* progress along the Christian path of discipleship; as we learn and discover more about God and his teachings in Scripture so our judgement and values will alter – if, that is, we allow and give permission for it to happen. For this is always a co-operative growth, it is not just a case of God imposing his will or judgement. Often we hold back on areas of our life and behaviour, either because they are too painful, or because we do not want to relinquish the control of being able to justify and retain judgement on them.

Spiritual activity

Think about the areas of your life where you have not been entirely honest. This may relate to your tax return or your dealings with friends or work colleagues, for example.

- Have you compromised yourself by being less than honest?
- What has that done to your spiritual growth?

Prayer

Almighty God, without you we are not able to please you.
Mercifully grant that your Holy Spirit may in all things direct
and rule our hearts; through Jesus Christ our Lord.

(*Common Worship*, Collect for the Nineteenth
Sunday after Trinity)

3

Essentials for the journey

———•═•═•———

THE TWELFTH DAY

Being in Christ

Bible readings

'I am the vine; you are the branches. If a man remains in me
and I in him, he will bear much fruit; apart from me you can
do nothing. If anyone does not remain in me, he is like a branch
that is thrown away and withers; such branches are picked up,
thrown into the fire and burned. If you remain in me and my
words remain in you, ask whatever you wish, and it will be given
you. This is to my Father's glory, that you bear much fruit,
showing yourselves to be my disciples.'

(John 15.5–8)

But as surely as God is faithful, our message to you is not
'Yes' and 'No'. For the Son of God, Jesus Christ, who was preached
among you by me and Silas and Timothy, was not 'Yes' and 'No',
but in him it has always been 'Yes'. For no matter how many
promises God has made, they are 'Yes' in Christ. And so through
him the 'Amen' is spoken by us to the glory of God. Now it
is God who makes both us and you stand firm in Christ. He
anointed us, set his seal of ownership on us, and put his Spirit
in our hearts as a deposit, guaranteeing what is to come.

(2 Corinthians 1.18–22)

* * *

Jesus, in this well-known passage from John 15, gets very personal. The words 'I' and 'You' occur regularly throughout the text. The 'I' is Jesus and the 'You' is each one of us. The message is directed clearly to each disciple and states that our spiritual life is rooted only in Christ. St Paul frequently used the term 'in Christ', as we find in 2 Corinthians. The Christian faith – our faith – only has its reality in Christ. If you take Christ out of faith you are left with nothing of substance, and what is left over is only fit for throwing away. 'I am the vine; you are the branches,' says Jesus. No branch is separate from the central stem; a branch gets its life from the main stem, because it has no sustenance of its own and no point of belonging. Simply, it cannot exist by itself.

So it is with our faith, and yet most people do not see it that way. They regard their spiritual life as their own. They do not treat worship as essential because it does not fit in with their personal priorities. The sacraments of bread and wine do not feature as a regular part of their spiritual devotion, because the reality of Christ's sacrifice has not yet dawned on them. Reading the Bible and praying are not seen as disciplines to be taken seriously, because their religion is a 'do-it-yourself' enterprise. Thus, the common attitude that prevails is 'I am spiritually responsible for myself. I am an autonomous human being, self-sufficient to make my own personal judgement about what I consider to be spiritual priorities'. Jesus contradicts this view and says, 'I am the vine; you are the branches…apart from me you can do nothing.'

The fundamental part of our spiritual journey is a recognition that the power, energy and reality of faith come from being joined into Christ. There is no 'DIY' religion. Christianity is not a religion of personal choice but of personal obedience. You may choose to be a Christian, but from that point on you surrender your personal choice to the will and authority of God. A realization of that fact is an essential aspect of our discipleship. For if we are to grow and bear the spiritual fruit that is the will of God, we must remain rooted in the one who enables life itself. Our personal priority must be to realize the truth of what being 'in Christ' means in relation to every aspect of our lives. As God our Father desires to see the fruit of that reality come into being, so our will must be subject to the divine will that is continually seeking to make that fruit grow in us.

Spiritual activity

Take a house plant or a plant from the garden and cut off one of the branches. Place it beside a healthy and attractive flower. Make sure both are in a prominent place which can be easily viewed. Watch carefully what happens to the branch over the next few days, and reflect on the simple spiritual message of Christ from John 15. By placing the branch beside a healthy plant the contrast between life and death is clearly visible.

Prayer

Lord, in you we live and move and have our being. Without you there is no real life so draw us deeper into you, so that we may find the reality of life itself. Amen.

THE THIRTEENTH DAY

Loved by Christ

Bible readings

In all their distress he too was distressed, and the angel of his presence saved them. In his love and mercy he redeemed them; he lifted them up and carried them all the days of old. Yet they rebelled and grieved his Holy Spirit.

(Isaiah 63.9–10a)

And I pray that you, being rooted and established in love, may have power, together with all the saints, to grasp how wide and long and high and deep is the love of Christ, and to know this love that surpasses knowledge – that you may be filled to the measure of all the fullness of God.

(Ephesians 3.17b–19)

'As the Father has loved me, so have I loved you. Now remain in my love. My command is this: Love each other as I have loved you. Greater love has no-one than this, that he lay down his life for his friends. You are my friends if you do what I command.'

(John 15.9, 12–14)

* * *

At the heart of the Christian faith is a personal relationship with Jesus Christ. It is an 'I–you' relationship where Jesus says, 'I love you'. It is direct and clear. Jesus says, 'I have loved you'; either we refuse to believe him, or we accept the reality of the statement based on the evidence that is demonstrated to us. A personal realization of this awesome truth is an essential tenet of a journey of faith. But Jesus does not simply make the statement without supporting it with evidence. He makes that love tangible by showing it; if we want proof of the ultimate result of a person's love and friendship, then we see it in their action of sacrificing their life on our behalf. Of course, the implication of Jesus' words in John's Gospel is that that is exactly what he intends to do. It is in the Cross that we see the love of God supremely demonstrated.

One of my favourite stories, which I have always found deeply moving, is the true story of a young boy who had a beautiful and attractive mother. She was always caring and compassionate. However, the child was extremely sensitive about his mother's hands; they were very marked and scarred and he did not like her to touch him. So, whenever she tried to take him by the hand on the way to school or the shops, he would resist being held. His refusal caused his mother a great deal of heartache and pain. One day, however, his father decided that he was old enough to be told the truth about his mother's hands.

Sitting him down in the kitchen, he explained what had taken place. He told him that one day, when he was just beginning to crawl, his mother was looking after him in the lounge. The telephone rang, so she quickly went into the hall to answer the call, which took a little longer than she had anticipated. She was halfway through the conversation when she heard him screaming. She rushed back into the lounge and, to her horror, discovered that he had crawled up to the open fire, pushed away the fireguard and his clothes had begun to catch alight. In desperation she looked around the room to see if there was anything that could be used to put out the flames. Seeing nothing of use she ran over to him, grabbed him and patted out the flames with her own bare hands. As a result, they were permanently marked and scarred. When his father told him the truth of what had happened he said nothing. But as time went on his feelings about his mother's hands changed and he felt proud, because he realized that her nasty hands were a demonstration of how much she loved him.

Therefore, when we look at Christ on the Cross, we see the ultimate demonstration of love. We see in his hands and his feet the price of love that he was prepared to pay in order to rescue us and show his personal love. His words 'I love you' have real meaning and truth because he shows how far he was prepared to go to show that he really meant it. It is wonderful if a friend shows such sacrificial love, but an even greater wonder is when it is God himself who shows it. Then the implications are infinitely greater. St Paul realized the magnitude of this incredible truth when writing to the Christians at Ephesus. He understood that the love of Christ was of such enormity that a purely human knowledge could not fathom the depth of its reality. Yet his prayer was that they would have the power to comprehend the enormity of what was expressed by God in Christ. An essential part of our journey is a growing realization of this truth, which is the basis of our faith.

Spiritual activity

Today, at an appropriate point, say to your partner that you love him or her. Then, even if it involves something very simple, demonstrate it in a tangible way.

Prayer

Lord, thank you for your sacrificial love shown to us in Christ. Help me to comprehend the reality of your love, and deepen my appreciation for the magnitude of what you have done for me. Amen.

THE FOURTEENTH DAY

Obedience to Christ

Bible readings

And now, O Israel, what does the Lord your God ask of you but to fear the Lord your God, to walk in all his ways, to love him, to serve the Lord your God with all your heart and with all your soul, and to observe the Lord's commands and decrees that I am giving you today for your own good?

(Deuteronomy 10.12–13)

'Now fear the Lord and serve him with all faithfulness. Throw away the gods your forefathers worshipped beyond the River and in Egypt, and serve the Lord. But if serving the Lord seems undesirable to you, then choose for yourselves this day whom you will serve, whether the gods your forefathers served beyond the River, or the gods of the Amorites, in whose land you are living. But as for me and my household, we will serve the Lord.'

(Joshua 24.14–15)

If you obey my commands, you will remain in my love, just as I have obeyed my Father's commands and remain in his love. This is my command: Love each other.

(John 15.10, 17)

* * *

The Christian writer Kenneth Leech said that Christianity goes wrong when Jesus is worshipped and not followed, which brings us to the heart of the issue of what it is to be a Christian. A Christian is not simply a good or a nice person who adopts middle-class English values. When talking to people about spiritual matters, and when questioning their views, some will become defensive; often criticizing other people, while justifying the good life that they themselves lead. But Christianity cannot be espoused on good moral behaviour alone. Why? Because

41

to be a Christian is to be a follower of Jesus Christ and his teachings. Sadly, the majority of people in Britain today have distorted that truth to suit a more convenient, personal view that justifies themselves and their actions purely on a level of being helpful to others.

At the heart of our faith is obedience: obedience to Jesus' teachings. Jesus makes demands that many would see as unreasonable – he asks us to change our priorities and lifestyle; he wants us to adopt a different value system that puts him first; he wants us to love others as much as we love ourselves.

This brings us back to Kenneth Leech's remark, which holds so much truth for us. It is not good enough to be entertained by choosing a form of religious expression that suits our background and own psychological disposition, for then it can so easily become idolatry, worshipping what we like. The faith of a believer demands the following of one person only, and that person is Christ. It involves being challenged and, at times, threatened by his teaching. It involves being prepared to reorder our lifestyle priorities so that he is at the centre of our world.

We will never grow and be gifted in our Christian life unless we are prepared to surrender and obey the new power that demands our observance. This is an obedience that costs, because it inevitably comes into conflict with our own desires and wishes. It is a painful path – to pretend otherwise is only the counsel of fools. If Jesus' obedience to his Father's will cost him his life, what makes us believe that it will be a convenient and easy process for us? What makes us think that our faith and Christian pilgrimage will not cost us money, status and personal pain? But just as a soldier who does not obey commands is no use to the army, so a Christian who does not have a heart of obedience will never be of use in the service of God. It is useless to express a desire that God should work in and through us, if we are not prepared to conform to what he demands of us. We cannot enjoy the thrill of closeness to

God and the power of his Holy Spirit, without the humility of acknowledging a higher authority and without complying with that authority with all our heart, soul and mind.

The essential attribute for our journey of Christian faith is to recognize our dependence on Christ, acknowledging his love for us and conforming to his teaching, so that we can grow into the complete person that he wants us to be.

Spiritual activity

Consider the question, 'Is there any area of my life that does not conform to the will of God or does not respond in obedience to God's ways?' If there is, how are you going to bring this area of your life into the arena of obedience to God?

Prayer

> *Almighty and Everlasting God,*
> *increase in us your gift of faith;*
> *that, forsaking what lies behind*
> *and reaching out to that which is before,*
> *we may run the way of your commandments*
> *and win the crown of everlasting joy;*
> *through Jesus Christ our Lord.*
> (*The Alternative Service Book 1980*)

THE FIFTEENTH DAY

A friend of Christ

Bible readings

Now Moses used to take a tent and pitch it outside the camp some distance away, calling it the 'tent of meeting'. Anyone enquiring of the Lord would go to the tent of meeting outside the camp. And whenever Moses went out to the tent, all the people rose and stood at the entrances to their tents, watching Moses until he entered the tent. As Moses went into the tent, the pillar of cloud would come down and stay at the entrance, while the Lord spoke with Moses. Whenever the people saw the pillar of cloud standing at the entrance to the tent, they all stood and worshipped, each at the entrance to his tent. The Lord would speak to Moses face to face, as a man speaks with his friend.

(Exodus 33.7–11)

I no longer call you servants, because a servant does not know his master's business. Instead, I have called you friends, for everything that I learned from my Father I have made known to you.

(John 15.15)

* * *

Friends are the most valuable dimension of life that we enjoy. There is nothing more agonizing than to be without friends, unable to communicate what we feel with another human being. When I was single, my friends kept me from going insane. There were four special friends who I could call on; they were always pleased to see me, even if I arrived unannounced. There were no conditions on the relationship – they were happy to listen, understand and offer encouragement when it was needed. Those friends have been present at the most important moments in my life, and I am sure they will still be friends at the end of my life.

44

The great aspect of marriage is that your partner becomes your best friend – the one who you can communicate with about the trivial and the crucially important matters of life. You know that the relationship you have with that person is different, because the level of communication is deeper and more powerful than you have ever experienced before. It gives you the conviction that this relationship is for life and is unique. The art then is to keep the channels of communication open, and not let complacency set in so that you stop listening and responding to one another.

How is it, then, that God offers his friendship to us? Friendship and intimacy are such vital parts of life, and yet God comes and says 'I have called you friends.' Why does the divine creator and sustainer of the universe, the person of awesome power and authority, give his friendship to us?

I remember walking some years ago along the river bank with my two-year-old son, Alastair. We stopped for a few moments to watch a couple with two young girls feed the ducks that had congregated by the side of the river. As we were watching, the mother suddenly turned to me and offered Alastair some bread so that he could also feed the ducks. I had never set eyes on the family before and there was no reason why she would have known me. Yet for no other reason than pure kindness she took the initiative and, as an act of friendship, offered the bread to him.

God takes the initiative with us for no other reason than pure love. Christ offers us his friendship; he wants to communicate with us since communication is at the very heart of friendships. Jesus has made known to us the person of God our Father. He has shown us what the Father is like. He has introduced us! An essential part of our spiritual journey is deepening and enjoying all that this vital friendship means.

When Jesus says to us 'I have called you friends', what more significant and powerful words overloaded with meaning could he have uttered? There is no excuse for us not to know Christ, because he is our friend.

Spiritual activity

Today, take the initiative and either with someone you know, or someone you have never met before, express to them an act of friendship. If you get the chance, reflect on how it made you feel, and the reaction you received from the person concerned.

Prayer

Lord, I thank you for my friends. When I am confused they give me wisdom. When I feel sad they help me smile. When I feel worthless they share their love. Lord, above all this, I thank you that you are my friend for ever. Amen.

THE SIXTEENTH DAY

Chosen by Christ

Bible readings

> Blessed is the nation whose God is the Lord,
> the people he chose for his inheritance.
> From heaven the Lord looks down and sees all mankind;
> from his dwelling-place he watches all who live on earth –
> he who forms the hearts of all, who considers everything
>   they do.
>
> (Psalm 33.12–15)

> You did not choose me, but I chose you to go and bear fruit –
> fruit that will last. Then the Father will give you whatever you
> ask in my name.
>
> (John 15.16)

> But we ought always to thank God for you, brothers loved by
> the Lord, because from the beginning God chose you to be saved
> through the sanctifying work of the Spirit and through belief
> in the truth. He called you to this through our gospel, that you
> might share in the glory of our Lord Jesus Christ. So then,
> brothers, stand firm and hold to the teachings we passed on to
> you, whether by word of mouth or by letter.
>
> (2 Thessalonians 2.13–15)

* * *

It hit me like a ton of bricks. I had not been expecting it. It
was unsettling; it completely changed my priorities and direction. I sat in my school study on that Saturday morning before
breakfast, and the words 'Why not the Church?' struck me
forcefully.

Until that moment, I had been considering social work as
a career, because I felt it was a practical way of helping people.
I was keeping my options open, however, and was thinking
seriously about a career in teaching or, possibly, the navy. Some
friends had suggested ordination, but I frankly did not think

of it as an attractive idea. I considered myself to be too normal a person to be straitjacketed into the role of a clergyman. But God had different ideas and he was going to overcome my prejudices. The more I thought about the words 'Why not the Church?', the more I realized that God had spoken forcefully to my thoughts, and that was exactly what he wanted me to do. He had chosen me to serve his Church as an ordained priest.

It is wonderful to think that God has no favourites – he chooses everyone and asks us to work for his Church and his world. In the first place, he chooses us to acknowledge and worship him as Lord. Then he chooses us to get to work in his world and for his people. Whether you are a clergyperson or an accountant, a road sweeper or an estate agent – it makes no difference. If you are doing the job that God has called you to do, then you are in the right place doing the right thing.

Some people incorrectly think that God calls some and not others, as if God is a divine lottery: some people's number comes up and they become Christians, and others' do not. This way of thinking creates a God who chooses his favourites and throws away the rest, a view that is totally unbiblical. As God expresses it, the nature of choice is that he takes the first step. He chooses to redeem mankind and to offer us a way back to himself; that choice he offers to everyone. We are all chosen because he has demonstrated his offer of forgiveness and the restoration of our relationship with him.

An essential part of our journey of faith is recognizing that God himself has chosen us. We may not play a prominent part in the life of our church or community, but he has chosen us to be the Christian presence just where we are: in our family situation, and in the road in which we live, for example. It is as simple and as vital as that.

Spiritual activity

Think for a few moments of the benefits of being a Christian. List them, if you wish, on a piece of paper. What are the good things that God has chosen to give you because you are his child?

Prayer

Father, thank you that out of your great love you have chosen me. You took the initiative and made it possible for me to have access into your presence. Help me to know your will and conform to all your purposes for my life. Amen.

THE SEVENTEENTH DAY

Adopted by Christ

Bible readings

For you did not receive a spirit that makes you a slave again to fear, but you have received the Spirit of sonship. And by him we cry, '*Abba*, Father.' The Spirit himself testifies with our spirit that we are God's children. Now if we are God's children, then we are heirs – heirs of God and co-heirs with Christ, if indeed we share in his sufferings in order that we may also share in his glory.

(Romans 8.15–17)

For he chose us in him before the creation of the world to be holy and blameless in his sight. In love he predestined us to be adopted as his sons through Jesus Christ, in accordance with his pleasure and will – to the praise of his glorious grace, which he has freely given us in the One he loves. In him we have redemption through his blood, the forgiveness of sins, in accordance with the riches of God's grace that he lavished on us with all wisdom and understanding.

(Ephesians 1.4–8)

* * *

Pregnancy is not always planned. If a couple find that they are expecting a baby which they had not intended, then – apart from the shock – there needs to be a whole period of readjustment which, at times, may not be easy to deal with. That does not mean to say that the child, when it is born, will not be loved and valued. It is not uncommon for couples who have two children and have decided that they are happy with that number to suddenly discover 'number three' is on the way!

God says that his intention for our adoption as his children was not a mistake, it was something he planned and predicted.

In fact, it was his pleasure and will. He wanted to do it because it was a natural and instinctive thing for a parent to do; it was his desire and joy. In other words, he was totally committed to what he was doing, both in heart and mind. As his adopted children, born of the Spirit, we are so able to know the intimacy of that personal relationship that we call God, 'Father'. The word 'Abba' in Aramaic has a less formal meaning to it than 'father', but is better translated as 'daddy'. 'Daddy' expresses a warmth and a closeness, and this is the kind of depth and affection that we can enjoy in our relationship with God. This closeness is offered to us – it does not have to be earned or striven for by our own efforts. It is given to us as a gift from our Father. The benefits, however, do not stop there; we find that – through adoption – God also offers to us forgiveness so that we are holy and blameless in his sight. We are no longer hostages to our own sin because that has been washed away through the blood of the one he sent to be our Saviour. All this he planned to do for us. It was not an afterthought or mistake, it was what he wanted.

A Christian is no longer an orphan but a child – a child of God. Before faith there was no personal knowledge of God. You may have known about him but you did not know him as a person, as a Father. But God offered to make you his child, to adopt you into that secure relationship and become part of the largest family on earth. Because of sin we are not naturally born to faith. Disobedience has separated us from God and broken the relationship. But God has offered us the opportunity to return. He promises to restore that which was destroyed and was no longer a natural relationship. Therefore, we are in a very privileged position, because we can receive all the benefits that come with our position as children. God is no longer the distant, shadowy figure obscured by mystery, he is our intimate parent who, through our relationship, offers knowledge of himself.

Spiritual activity

Spend a few minutes listing what the word 'daddy' means to you. Then, looking at your list, ask yourself whether those concepts are descriptive of your relationship with God your loving Father.

Prayer

Father, thank you for adopting me into your family and for giving me a knowledge of yourself. Help me to draw closer to you and experience the intimacy that I can discover as a child of God. Amen.

4

Fit for the road

———•◦•———

THE EIGHTEENTH DAY

God's Spirit

Bible readings

Then he said to me: 'Son of man, these bones are the whole house of Israel. They say, "Our bones are dried up and our hope is gone; we are cut off." Therefore prophesy and say to them: "This is what the Sovereign Lord says: O my people, I am going to open your graves and bring you up from them; I will bring you back to the land of Israel. Then you, my people, will know that I am the Lord, when I open your graves and bring you up from them. I will put my Spirit in you and you will live, and I will settle you in your own land. Then you will know that I the Lord have spoken, and I have done it," declares the Lord.'

(Ezekiel 37.11–14)

As soon as Jesus was baptized, he went up out of the water. At that moment heaven was opened, and he saw the Spirit of God descending like a dove and lighting on him. And a voice from heaven said, 'This is my Son, whom I love: with him I am well pleased.'

(Matthew 3.16–17)

Such confidence as this is ours through Christ before God. Not that we are competent to claim anything for ourselves, but our competence comes from God. He has made us competent as ministers of a new covenant – not of the letter but of the Spirit; for the letter kills, but the Spirit gives life.

(2 Corinthians 3.4–6)

* * *

You do not need a degree in theology to understand the clear message of what is contained in the Bible in terms of the work of God's Spirit. In the Old Testament, God gave his Spirit to special people at certain times to fulfil particular tasks. Yet within the Old Testament there was an anticipation of the time when God would give his Spirit to *all* his children. His children would then possess the fullness of the reality of the promises of God. With Jesus we find the same, clear message: that without the Spirit of God, the task and the calling will not be fulfilled. Before his baptism, Christ exercised no public ministry. He did not perform the task that God had called him to because he was not in receipt of the ability to do so. Yet it was his baptism and the coming of the Spirit upon him that gave him the power and ability to live out his call from God.

This was true of the early Church, in a vivid and dramatic way. After Jesus' crucifixion, the disciples were confused and unsure of what to do. Despite having encountered the Risen Christ, they did not have the ability and power to realize what God was calling them to do. All that changed with the coming of the Holy Spirit at the day of Pentecost. The transformation was shattering. Gone were the weak and indecisive followers, who were beginning to return to their old jobs before they met Christ. Heralded in were the renewed disciples, who knew what task God was calling them to and what ability they had been given to fulfil that reality.

The Spirit of God is critical to our discipleship. If we, as pilgrims, are going to be fit for the road ahead, and able to complete any task, we need to be filled with the Spirit, because the way is beyond human resources. We need the unlimited resources of God and his Spirit. We dare not have the arrogance and complacency to think that we can do things without the help and power of the Spirit. The Old Testament characters could not work without the Spirit, Jesus did not work without the Spirit, and the Church owed its very birth to the coming of the Spirit. So the message is clear: we need to receive and be filled with God's Spirit. How do you receive – by simply asking and obeying? You ask God to fill you with the Spirit, and then you keep your allegiance to his commands.

The pilgrim's acts of asking and obeying go hand in hand, because without asking you cannot receive, and without obeying you cannot be filled. The wonderful news is that God is more than willing to impart his Spirit to us, to give us that life which brings us back from the dead and that transforms the dry emptiness of the purely physical and rational human side of our life. Equipped with the Spirit we can move forward on our journey. We are competent to tackle the road ahead.

Spiritual activity

Reflect on the significant events in your life in terms of your Christian growth, particularly the times when you made real progress in your understanding of faith.

- Are you able to discern the part that the Holy Spirit had to play in your growth?
- What lessons can you learn from that experience?

Prayer

Come Holy Spirit, and fill my life. Breathe your divine reality into me. Equip and enable me to fulfil your tasks so that I may follow you, the Risen Ascended Lord. Amen.

THE NINETEENTH DAY

Discovery

Bible readings

At that time Jesus said, 'I praise you, Father, Lord of heaven and earth, because you have hidden these things from the wise and learned, and revealed them to little children. Yes, Father, for this was your good pleasure. All things have been committed to me by my Father. No one knows the Son except the Father, and no one knows the Father except the Son and those to whom the Son chooses to reveal him. Come to me, all you who are weary and burdened, and I will give you rest. Take my yoke upon you and learn from me, for I am gentle and humble in heart, and you will find rest for your souls. For my yoke is easy and my burden is light.'

(Matthew 11.25–30)

But when he, the Spirit of truth, comes, he will guide you into all truth. He will not speak of his own; he will speak only what he hears, and he will tell you what is yet to come. He will bring glory to me by taking from what is mine and making it known to you.

(John 16.13–14)

* * *

Part of the excitement of travel is the discovery of new things, whether they be people or places or colours or tastes. An often-quoted phrase is, 'travel broadens the mind'. Why is it, then, that Christians – in travelling the spiritual journey – often become narrow-minded and fail to discover the deeper realities of God? The Christian path must be a journey of discovery which involves revealing more about ourselves and, particularly, more about the ways and purposes of God. So often we inhibit our discovery by our own prejudices and presuppositions. We limit God to our known experiences, and fail to recognize him when he endeavours to break through and teach us facets of the truth that, as yet, we know nothing about.

Jesus praised the children but condemned the wise and learned. The reason is quite simple: children are willing to learn and discover. You only have to see your own or other people's children to recognize this. For them, the simple things which we take for granted become sources of great interest. When our two boys were young, we were constantly surprised at the seemingly uninteresting objects which took on a tremendous fascination for them; whether it was a stone, a leaf or a beetle, they had the joy of approaching everything with a spirit of discovery and wonder. The wise and learned, however, are those who think they know it all, and have lost their sense of awe and amazement.

Jesus, on the other hand, encourages us to learn about him and here we are assisted by the Holy Spirit, who actually makes known the ways of Christ to us. Therefore, we must not limit our understanding of God to our intellectual knowledge and confined experience alone. How can we say that we know the meaning of all that Jesus teaches, and have fully understood the implications of his words for our lives? We must employ a spirit of discovery if our journey is going to lead us on, and if we are going to be open to the deeper call of God on our lives. The Spirit is able to illuminate more of the truth about ourselves and about God, so that we are able to grow in holiness and be filled with a greater spiritual beauty and truth.

One of the most exciting and risky actions you can take is to say to God that your life is at his disposal, that you are prepared to obey his call on your life – whatever that call may be. It is risky – God may just take you at your word because he needs you to serve in a part of his kingdom. You may have to give up a great deal of what you had come to value, but joy will come in the discovery that, by obedience to his will, you have uncovered a deeper and more profound trust in him.

Spiritual activity

Write down those areas of the Christian faith that you have learnt about over the past six months. They may include certain biblical details as well as aspects of trust in God that you have discovered for yourself.

Prayer

Lord, take my life; let it be wholly consecrated, Lord, to thee. Amen.

THE TWENTIETH DAY

Changing

Bible readings

So Jacob said to his household and to all who were with him, 'Get rid of the foreign gods you have with you, and purify yourselves and change your clothes. Then come, let us go up to Bethel, where I will build an altar to God, who answered me in the days of my distress and who has been with me wherever I have gone.'

(Genesis 35.2–3)

'I the Lord do not change.'

(Malachi 3.6a)

Listen, I tell you a mystery: We will not all sleep, but we will all be changed – in a flash, in the twinkling of an eye, at the last trumpet. For the trumpet will sound, the dead will be raised imperishable, and we will be changed. For the perishable must clothe itself with the imperishable, and the mortal with immortality. When the perishable has been clothed with the imperishable, and the mortal with immortality, then the saying that is written will come true: 'Death has been swallowed up in victory.'

(1 Corinthians 15.51–54)

* * *

All of us have aspects of our lives or the world that we would like to change. Some may be rather petty; others may have consequences that would alter our lives for ever. For example, I would rather like to have Christmas changed so that it falls on a Sunday every year. It takes place on December 25th because originally it was a popular pagan festival which the Church adopted as a convenient date to celebrate Jesus' birth. But my reason for wanting to change it is rather selfish: it would make Christmas less of a manic experience from a clergyman's point of view. I would also like to change my car to a newer model, but I cannot afford to at the moment.

Just recently, a very dear friend whom I have known for many years revealed something which drew us to love her with a greater compassion and understanding. I should say that this friend is one of the most beautiful people I have ever met. She has such a warmth and love for others, combined with a glowing faith, that you feel it is an honour to know her. She told us that when she was 18 she had a baby which was immediately offered for adoption. All her life she had kept it a secret; no one knew except her late husband. However, not long ago she decided that she had to find out what had happened to her son. She tracked him down, and discovered that he was married with two lovely children. She then introduced him to her two daughters, and the whole thing was a very moving and powerful experience.

Some circumstances, though, we cannot change, and we find it difficult to accept the impact they have on us for the rest of our lives. There may be some areas that we want to keep exactly the same. We have got used to doing things in a certain way and are very reluctant to see that altered. Rationality often disappears, and the issue quickly gets lost in subjective and emotive arguments. Any change, whether we judge it to be for good or bad, requires a certain amount of readjustment, and that is often the reason why we may be reluctant to accept it.

However, a pilgrim people who are disciples of Jesus Christ must be people who are open to change. We are called to change because God is changeless. He is the Almighty King, unadulterated in love and purity. He does not need to change because he is complete. Yet it is we who are imperfect and flawed, and therefore need to change. A Christian who resists growth, and who has an inability to cope with spiritual development and change, has not grasped the fact that our change is a continuous process. It commences at a spiritual level when we begin to acknowledge and worship God, and continues on until the day – in the eternal purposes of God – we shall be changed from our perishable humanity to the imperishable that God shall bestow on us. But before that moment we are in transition, aspiring to what God would have us be, and withdrawing from the things which spoil and disfigure our witness.

Spiritual activity

Consider those areas in your life which you wish to change: the areas where you have failed and have had to come to terms with the consequences, or the defects in your personality which reflect badly on yourself, your family and your faith. Having acknowledged these aspects, consider what you may do to alter their influence, accepting the grace of God to change for the better.

Prayer

> *God, give us grace to accept with serenity*
> *the things that cannot be changed,*
> *courage to change the things that should be changed,*
> *and the wisdom to distinguish the one from the other.*
> (Reinhold Niebuhr)

THE TWENTY-FIRST DAY

Renewing

Bible readings

Create in me a pure heart, O God,
and renew a steadfast spirit within me.

(Psalm 51.10)

Do you not know? Have you not heard? The Lord is the everlasting God, the Creator of the ends of the earth. He will not grow tired or weary, and his understanding no one can fathom. He gives strength to the weary and increases the power of the weak. Even youths grow tired and weary, and young men stumble and fall; but those who hope in the Lord will renew their strength. They will soar on wings like eagles: they will run and not grow weary, they will walk and not be faint.

(Isaiah 40.28–31)

Therefore, I urge you, brothers, in view of God's mercy, to offer your bodies as living sacrifices, holy and pleasing to God – this is your spiritual act of worship. Do not conform any longer to the pattern of this world, but be transformed by the renewing of your mind. Then you will be able to test and approve what God's will is – his good, pleasing and perfect will.

(Romans 12.1–2)

* * *

Renewal is a common experience for us all. We do it all the time, whether it be renewing the subscription to a magazine or membership of an organization, or restoring an item back to its original working condition. The word 'renew', according to *The Oxford Illustrated Dictionary*, means to restore to its original state, to make as good as new or to patch up or regenerate. So its meaning can be applied in a variety of ways; likewise, that applies to the way it is used in the Bible, because we find its meaning used to indicate that renewal can happen in a number of ways. There is the renewal of our strength, our spirits and our minds. This is a very potent combination, and it makes you realize that our faith touches us at the essential points of life. As a pilgrim people we look to God – he is the one who can affect the fundamental regeneration that takes our mind and our spirit, renews them, and elevates them to the places we can only hope to reach.

Of course, we would be fools to think that this is an easy process that happens in an instant. We may be so immersed in the superficial and transient values of the society in which we live that we have to learn the values of Christ. While some of us may be dramatically converted, it can take others some time to work through a change of values and spiritual priorities. The reason for this is that we need to sit at the feet of Christ, and learn from him, so that our minds are renewed with the values of the Kingdom of God. Sometimes our renewal will be so slow and gradual that it is only in looking back over the months and years that we realize that a change has come about. Maybe our sexual fantasies are giving way to purer thoughts, or our desire for greater financial wealth is moving further down our list of worries and priorities. If we give God permission he will renew us, and he will use us to do things we never thought possible. He also will give us the strength to go on, and that strength will not be a human strength, but rather one which comes from God's Holy Spirit.

Nicholas Halasz, however, tells the story of a renewal of mind and priorities that was unexpected and very dramatic. Alfred Nobel, the inventor of dynamite, awoke one morning in 1888 to read his own obituary. It had been printed as a result of a simple journalistic error – his brother had died, and a French reporter carelessly reported the death of Alfred instead. Any man would naturally be disturbed under the circumstances, but to Nobel the shock was overwhelming. He saw himself as the world saw him – 'the dynamite King', the great industrialist who had made his immense fortune from explosives. This, as far as the general public was concerned, was the entire purpose of his life. None of his true intentions – to break down the barriers that separated men and ideas – were recognized and given serious consideration. He was quite simply a merchant of death, and for that alone he would be remembered. Nobel resolved to make clear the true meaning and purpose of his life. This could be done through the final disposition of his fortune. His will would be the expression of his life's ideals. The result, the annual Nobel peace prize, is the most valued of prizes, given to those who have done the most for the cause of world peace.

Spiritual activity

Look back over whatever period of time you think is appropriate, and consider which of your values, priorities, thought patterns and general aspects of life have been renewed because of the teachings of Christ, and the activity of the Holy Spirit in your life. Then ask yourself what other areas need to be renewed so that they conform to the way of Christ.

Prayer

Father, I am wholly yours. Come with the renewing power of your Holy Spirit, and restore in me the mind and strength of spirit that you alone can bring. Rejuvenate within me the right values that come from a mind that knows your ways. Amen.

THE TWENTY-SECOND DAY

Empowering

Bible readings

Come and see what God has done,
how awesome his works on man's behalf!
He turned the sea into dry land,
they passed through the river on foot –
come, let us rejoice in him.
He rules for ever by his power,
his eyes watch the nations –
let not the rebellious rise up against him.

(Psalm 66.5–7)

On one occasion, while he was eating with them, he gave them this command: 'Do not leave Jerusalem, but wait for the gift my Father promised, which you have heard me speak about. For John baptized with water, but in a few days you will be baptized with the Holy Spirit.' So when they met together, they asked him, 'Lord, are you at this time going to restore the kingdom of Israel?' He said to them: 'It is not for you to know the times or dates the Father has set by his own authority. But you will receive power when the Holy Spirit comes on you; and you will be my witnesses in Jerusalem, and in all Judea and Samaria, and to the ends of the earth.'

(Acts 1.4–8)

I pray also that the eyes of your heart may be enlightened in order that you may know the hope to which he has called you, the riches of his glorious inheritance in the saints, and his incomparably great power for us who believe. That power is like the working of his mighty strength, which he exerted in Christ when he raised him from the dead and seated him at the right hand in the heavenly realms.

(Ephesians 1.18–21)

* * *

A few years ago Hilary and I went to Paris for a weekend. We had booked into a hotel which was within walking distance of most of the main attractions in the centre of that beautiful city. We arrived early on the Friday afternoon and, after unpacking our bags, decided to wander through the streets up to the Sacré Coeur, that magnificent church perched at the top of the Montmartre district. Despite the fact that it was March and, therefore, not the height of the tourist season, the church was flooded with visitors from all over the world. Its popularity was in many ways distracting. It was really too crowded to be able to convey a sense of spiritual serenity and worship. Yet, not to be put off, we wandered around the building taking in the sights and religious features.

When we had finished, we noticed that there was a sign up behind the chairs in front of the altar which simply said, 'Reserved for Prayer'. There were quite a few people sitting there quietly praying despite the general noise. We had not noticed them or the sign when we entered, since we were being carried along by the crowd. So we decided to stop for a few moments and pray. No sooner had we sat down, than we felt a tremendous sense of the power and presence of God. It was like being physically gripped by a force which was strong and yet beautifully moving and reassuring. Part of our reaction was a desire to shout to all our fellow tourists and encourage them to come in and experience the same power of the presence of God. It was very moving, particularly because the sensation was so unexpected. We did not want to leave, but eventually we departed with a deep sense of joy and wonder.

The Bible talks a lot about power but, of course, the focus of that power is in the hands of God. He is the source of all power and the one who gives power to his people. That power comes from the sanctifying and renewing work of the Holy Spirit. The Spirit, which is the same Spirit which brought Christ back from the dead, is in and at work in every believing, baptized Christian. That is God's promise. But the Spirit is not given for our own personal gratification, or to enhance our personal power. The Spirit is given so that we may serve and witness for Jesus. We are given the strength and ability to live the life of faith, because we have no power to do it ourselves. If you are attempting the Christian pilgrimage in your own strength, you will never complete it, and you certainly will never be fit for the road. The good news, however, is that God empowers his people to follow that path. At some points in our lives we may be very aware of the power of the presence of God, and those experiences serve as reminders of the constant reality that God's power is leading us on.

Spiritual activity

- What have been the times in your own Christian experience when you have been particularly aware of the power and presence of God?
- How did those experiences help you to grasp and develop your understanding of what God wanted you to do in his service?
- What power do you need now to overcome the challenges and difficulties you face as an individual, a family and as part of your church congregation?

Prayer

Come Holy Spirit, and empower me with your strength to live my Christian life. Give me the necessary gifts to fulfil my purpose while I am here on earth. Lord, use me in the service of your Kingdom, and equip me with your divine power of goodness, truth and self-sacrifice. Amen.

THE TWENTY-THIRD DAY

Peace

Bible readings

The Lord said to Moses, 'Tell Aaron and his sons, "This is how you are to bless the Israelites. Say to them: 'The Lord bless you and keep you; the Lord make his face shine upon you and be gracious to you; the Lord turn his face towards you and give you peace.'"'

(Numbers 6.22–26)

May the God of hope fill you with all joy and peace as you trust in him, so that you may overflow with hope by the power of the Holy Spirit.

(Romans 15.13)

'All this I have spoken while still with you. But the Counsellor, the Holy Spirit, whom the Father will send in my name, will teach you all things and will remind you of everything I have said to you. Peace I leave with you; my peace I give you. I do not give to you as the world gives. Do not let your hearts be troubled and do not be afraid.'

(John 14.25–27)

* * *

A psychiatrist once remarked, 'With peace in his soul a man can face the most terrifying experiences. But without peace in his soul he cannot manage even as simple a task as writing a letter.' There is no doubt about it: peace of mind is a very important part of life. When we are worried or troubled, each of us tends to respond in our own particular way. Some of us will lie awake at night, others will get headaches, or become bad-tempered; all these reactions are ordinary symptoms of worry and stress. Naturally, one person can be troubled by an experience or concern that would not disturb another person at all. We all recognize that we react in different ways.

Jesus speaks to us about a peace which is not the panacea that remedies all the worries and stress that the world and life throw at us, but rather a peace that equips us for the road ahead. It is a peace that is not available anywhere else, because Christ alone bestows it on his followers. He promises us that peace and therefore he can be relied on to give it, yet we need to *accept* it. God cannot be blamed if you or I do not possess his spiritual peace; he takes the initiative and offers it to us, it is then up to us to receive it.

Where does that peace come from? Well, it comes from a number of things. Firstly, it comes from responding to God. It is pointless to expect peace if we are living contrary to God's teachings and purposes for our lives. The philosopher Dante wrote, 'In his will is our peace.' And if we are not following God's will we will not find his peace. In fact, that sense of peace is often an excellent guide to discover what is the will of God, if we are in doubt. Of course, God's will is discovered through his teaching in the Bible, but when we have an important decision to make, it is crucial to be receptive to a sense of peace about what is right or wrong. You will recall me mentioning that before I thought about being ordained, I seriously considered social work as a practical way of helping others. However, as I said, I never felt a great sense of peace about it. It was only when I felt called to ordination that I had a deep sense of peace about the path God wanted me to follow. At the time I did not realize it, but it was God's way of trying to tell me what was right and what was not his will.

Secondly, peace comes from obedience to God. George Eliot said, 'I could not live in peace if I put the shadow of a wilful sin between myself and God.' If our lifestyle does not reflect obedience to the moral and spiritual teachings of Christ, then we will not perceive the peace that Christ offers to us. However, when we seek to discover his will and conform to his teachings in terms of our priorities, values and morality, then we can know the peace that transcends the illusory satisfactions of doing what we want.

Thirdly, peace comes from a real trust in God. Often we are tempted to retreat into a human anxiety or worry because we are unable to control our situations and circumstances. The focus of our thoughts and perceptions is consigned too much to the priorities of self and the world, and not of God. At that point we need to look beyond ourselves and our personal circumstances to the one who ultimately holds everything in his hands. He is the one who can be trusted for all of life and death, and there is nothing that can obscure his love and concern for us.

The Christian path and road which we follow is not easy. Jesus never said it would be. But if we live out our lives with the strength of the peace of knowing and following him, we will reach the fulfilment of all his promises for us.

Spiritual activity

At some point today, when you have the opportunity, go into a quiet part of your house or flat and light a candle. Observe it for a few minutes, looking at the shape and form of the flame. Allow yourself to forget about your anxieties and concerns. Focus your thoughts on Jesus, and then quietly say to yourself, 'Peace I leave with you; my peace I give you'. Repeat this phrase many times until you are still inside. Then recall what concerns you, and ask God to share with you in those concerns. Finally, when you are ready, blow out the candle.

Prayer

May the peace of God, which passes all understanding, keep our hearts and minds in the knowledge and love of God, and of his Son Jesus Christ. And may the blessing of God Almighty, the Father, and the Son and the Holy Spirit, be with us all. Amen.

5

Distractions on the way

THE TWENTY-FOURTH DAY

Not good enough

Bible readings

One day, after Moses had grown up, he went out to where his own people were and watched them at their hard labour. He saw an Egyptian beating a Hebrew, one of his own people. Glancing this way and that and seeing no one, he killed the Egyptian and hid his body in the sand.

(Exodus 2.11–12)

But Moses said to God, 'Who am I, that I should go to Pharaoh and bring the Israelites out of Egypt?'

(Exodus 3.11)

Moses said to the Lord, 'O Lord, I have never been eloquent, neither in the past nor since you have spoken to your servant. I am slow of speech and tongue.'

(Exodus 4.10)

In him and through faith in him we may approach God with freedom and confidence.

(Ephesians 3.12)

* * *

One of the most common excuses that everyone uses at some time or other is: 'Oh no, I could not possibly do that, *I would not be good enough.*' So often we can stifle our Christian growth, and

71

get distracted from the spiritual path of faith, by our excuses and feelings of inadequacy. We allow ourselves to abdicate responsibility and action for circumstances we know we should deal with, because we think that we have to obtain some particular standard of holiness before we could possibly attempt them. We also live under the illusion that the characters of the Bible are superheroes of faith, totally remote and isolated from our contemporary experience. The truth, however, is very different.

On closer examination, the heroes of the Bible are, in fact, very human, fallible characters. They show all sorts of weaknesses and unsuitability for the task which God calls them to. If the truth be known they are very like you and me. They had their doubts and lack of belief in themselves. No one was this more true of than Moses. If anyone was not good enough for the role of a leader of God's people, it was a murderer who was totally reluctant to take on the task for which God had so clearly called him. Moses repeatedly finds excuses not to obey God. Like most of us, his first appeal is to the fact that he is a nobody. Running through his mind, surely, was a lack of confidence in himself; after all, he probably still had an acute sense of guilt about the murder he had committed, which he thought he could carry out without detection. But he was found out. He had no credibility in the eyes of his own people, and possibly not much in his own. So with this dramatic encounter with God he just makes excuses: 'I am a nobody, they will not believe me, and I cannot speak very well in public.' And, in the end, he even has the audacity to say to God, 'O Lord, please send someone else to do it.'

What excuses do we use that distract us from the path that God has called us to follow? Those excuses that remain reasons for disobedience achieve nothing, and will not get us anywhere. Fortunately, Moses did – in the end – give up on his excuses and obey God. The result was that God used him in the most remarkable way, and achieved results which he could not have imagined.

The fact is that although we are all sinners and not good enough, we are forgiven, offered new life and a new start. I recently asked someone to assist with the cup at Communion, and his reply was that he was not a terribly good Christian. I said that if he realized that, then he was well qualified to assist, which he duly did.

As God's children we are well aware of our own inadequacies and weaknesses, but we can be confident, not in ourselves, but rather in the one who has called us on our Christian pilgrimage. After all, we are able to approach him with confidence because the secret of success – as Moses found out – is the fact that God is always with us. He will not let us down, so let us not deny him by contradicting what he can do in and through us.

Spiritual activity

List the areas of your life and faith where you have made excuses, or have declined to do something because you felt you were not good enough. Reflecting on that list, ask yourself whether you have denied God the opportunity to work through you because of your excuses. The question is, will you use the same excuse next time, and therefore be distracted from fulfilling the call and purpose of God in your life?

Prayer

Lord, help me to see that you are more than capable of making up for my own inadequacies. You, Lord, are the enabler and equipper, who gives good gifts to those who are called to follow you. Help me to put my faith in you, and not in myself. Amen.

THE TWENTY-FIFTH DAY

Fear

Bible readings

They said to Moses, 'Was it because there were no graves in Egypt that you brought us to the desert to die? What have you done to us by bringing us out of Egypt? Didn't we say to you in Egypt, "Leave us alone; let us serve the Egyptians?" It would have been better for us to serve the Egyptians than to die in the desert!' Moses answered the people, 'Do not be afraid. Stand firm and you will see the deliverance the Lord will bring you today. The Egyptians you see today you will never see again. The Lord will fight for you; you need only be still.'

(Exodus 14.11–14)

Immediately Jesus made the disciples get into the boat and go on ahead of him to the other side, while he dismissed the crowd. After he had dismissed them, he went up on a mountainside by himself to pray. When evening came, he was there alone, but the boat was already a considerable distance from land, buffeted by the waves because the wind was against it. During the fourth watch of the night Jesus went out to them, walking on the lake. When the disciples saw him walking on the lake, they were terrified. 'It's a ghost,' they said, and cried out in fear.

(Matthew 14.22–27)

When I saw him, I fell at his feet as though dead. Then he placed his right hand on me and said: 'Do not be afraid. I am the First and the Last. I am the Living One; I was dead, and behold I am alive for ever and ever! And I hold the keys of death and Hades.'

(Revelation 1.17–18)

* * *

Fear can paralyse. It can stop you in your tracks and hold you in its grip. For the Christian, fear can appear at many different levels. It can be the fear of the known as well as the unknown. For the children of Israel, fear was a very real and tangible sensation. They had an Egyptian army bearing down on them, threatening to annihilate them, or – at best – take them back to captivity. Fear clouded their judgement. They reckoned that they would have been better off remaining as slaves in Egypt. Instead of looking forward, all they could do was look back. Their attitude was not one of faith but of fear. Fortunately, Moses as a leader was a man who listened to God, and who knew what God was able to do. His vision of life was able to encompass more than just the circumstances around him. Sometimes we are distracted in our journey of faith, because of the fear that makes us see only ourselves and our own situation. It is then that we need to lift up our eyes and hold firm to the God whose power is beyond us, and who carries us through our difficulties. To do otherwise spells danger for ourselves and our faith.

While the children of Israel feared the known, the disciples feared the unknown. When they saw the Risen Lord they could not understand what was happening. It was outside their experience and it terrified them. They did not understand that it was the Lord himself walking towards them because their minds had told them that such an occurrence was not possible. But God is the God of all, and to him nothing is impossible. Sometimes, in our Christian faith, we can be held back by the fear of what we do not understand, and the fact is that there are many facets of God that are difficult to comprehend. But if we allow fear to inhibit our exploration and understanding of the mystery of God, we will never effectively journey along that road to deeper faith and fellowship with him.

Many Christians are fearful of the Holy Spirit, usually because they do not understand the person and the work of the Holy Spirit as part of the Trinity of God. Yet by being fearful, they quench what the Spirit wishes to do in and through them, and as a result they are impoverished.

A very moving story is told about the Rev. Hubert Pugh, a chaplain in the forces during the Second World War. He was on board a troop ship which was torpedoed, and as the ship was going down he was offered a place on one of the lifeboats. However, he declined; going to the hold of the rapidly sinking ship, he saw the packed lower decks full of men who had no hope of escape. He tied a coil of rope around his waist and asked a fellow officer to lower him into the hold, so that he could be with the men. When the officer protested, saying that he would surely perish, he replied, 'Believe me, my faith in God is far stronger than my fear of death at this moment.' Hubert Pugh went down with the ship. For this act of self-sacrifice he was posthumously awarded the George Cross.

Spiritual activity

Think for a moment about your fears: those which you know about, and those which you do not understand and, therefore, that hold you back from a deeper sense of trust in God. Being aware of these feelings, reflect on how you are going to bring together your faith and fears, so that faith overcomes.

- Will this involve more reading and learning?
- Are these matters that need to be discussed with your spiritual leaders?
- How are you going to make progress?

Prayer

Lord, lead me from fear to faith. Help me to overcome the fears which I would rather avoid because they frighten me. You know, Lord, that I do not understand and cannot fully comprehend in my limited experience of life. Help me to see as you see, and to have faith in you. Amen.

THE TWENTY-SIXTH DAY
Too hard a road

Bible readings

'Ah, Sovereign Lord, you have made the heavens and the earth by your great power and outstretched arm. Nothing is too hard for you. You show love to thousands but bring the punishment for the fathers' sins into the laps of their children after them. O great and powerful God, whose name is the Lord Almighty, great are your purposes and mighty are your deeds.'

(Jeremiah 32.17–19a)

The disciples were amazed at his words. But Jesus said again, 'Children, how hard it is to enter the kingdom of God! It is easier for a camel to go through the eye of a needle than for a rich man to enter the kingdom of God.'

(Mark 10.24–25)

Endure hardship with us like a good soldier of Christ Jesus. No one serving as a soldier gets involved in civilian affairs – he wants to please his commanding officer. Similarly, if anyone competes as an athlete, he does not receive the victor's crown unless he competes according to the rules. The hardworking farmer should be the first to receive a share of the crops. Reflect on what I am saying, for the Lord will give you insight into all this.

(2 Timothy 2.3–7)

* * *

Some tasks are so great that you look at the road ahead and think, 'I cannot do it, I will never get there.' The Christian life is not easy but Jesus never said it would be. Sometimes it can be so hard and painful that you feel you do not have the energy to carry on. What often distracts us are the difficulties we face, and we are not sure how to handle them.

The Christian faith and the journey we are on will go through dark patches. There will be times when we pray and nothing seems to happen. There will be no feeling or sense which comforts and encourages us. Our reading of the Bible seems lifeless, and we long to return to the time when it provided us with the inspiration to thrill and restore our spirits. Worship seems so cold and functional that we wonder why we bother to do it, why we go through the motions that seem so empty. Add to these hard times those periods of tragedy when we are angry with God, and we wonder why on earth he allows such awful things to happen.

At times, God also seems to demand more than we can give. The sacrifices we make stretch us to the limit of our endurance and we feel very exposed and vulnerable. I have felt that I was engaged in too much – trying to keep the faith and extend the kingdom – while not getting the back-up and support that I needed to keep going. I began to wonder whether the road was too hard. It is at points like this that it is very easy to get distracted, to focus on yourself and not on God. The obstacles may seem great, but each day is another step in overcoming the difficulties that may be in the way. We are often thrown into conflict, but that is what we signed up for – why should we expect anything else?

The path of obedience to God and following his call in our lives may get tough, and we may get worn down by the stress of it, but we are called to endure. The early Christians endured so much for their faith; our sufferings may be more subtle and indirect than theirs, and perhaps less obvious, but they are equally as real to us. However, passages such as Jeremiah 32.17–19a break upon us with such power and hope. They remind us that nothing is too hard for God; if he has promised to be with us, then we will not fail in what he has called us to do. We will not be overcome by the tasks before us or the difficulties that surround us.

Spiritual activity

Think for a moment of some of the difficulties that you have overcome in recent years. Possibly, these have been times when you felt like giving up. How did God lead you through those difficulties and hardships, and what are the lessons you learnt from those experiences?

Prayer

Lord, give me the strength of your Holy Spirit. When the road seems too hard and the difficulties too painful, give me the determination to soldier on. Help me to carry my cross in the knowledge that I do your will. I ask this through my Lord and Saviour, Jesus Christ. Amen.

THE TWENTY-SEVENTH DAY

Insecurities

Bible readings

'Yet if you devote your heart to him and stretch out your hands to him, if you put away the sin that is in your hand and allow no evil to dwell in your tent, then you will lift up your face without shame; you will stand firm without fear. You will surely forget your trouble, recalling it only as waters gone by. Life will be brighter than noonday, and darkness will become like morning. You will be secure, because there is hope; you will look about you and take your rest in safety.'

(Job 11.13–18)

We live by faith, not by sight.

(2 Corinthians 5.7)

* * *

No human being is totally secure about everything. All of us have weaknesses which make us feel very insecure. Some people appear very confident, in control of their life and what happens around them, but usually there will be a part of their life which they feel very insecure about; they will ignore it because they do not want to face it or deal with it. Some people may be very capable at their job, but when it comes to making conversation at a personal level just do not know what to say. Some may be capable of arguing their case at a meeting, but find that reading in public increases their anxiety levels dramatically. Others have a gift with facts and figures but, when it comes to standing up in public, would rather the ground swallowed them up than face a large crowd. Conversely, some people are not at all intimidated by addressing a large crowd, yet if asked to speak to a small group of half a dozen would become extremely stressed.

Sometimes the insecurities which affect each one of us are transferred to our faith, and cause us to become paralysed in our growth. The big question becomes 'What if...?'; we become frightened that God will ask us to do the one thing which, in our eyes, we are most incapable of doing. We can then carry that insecurity around with us, which in turn blocks us from the freedom of knowing the fullness of a growing faith. But, of course, the truth is that God would not ask us to do something which he would not equip us to accomplish. He is not a mean, small-minded person who gets some sort of pleasure out of making us feel insecure and vulnerable. He would never call us to do what we are most afraid of, without giving us all that we need to do that task. In fact, sometimes, in order to prove his power in our lives, God takes our weaknesses and encourages us to grow through them, so that we learn to be humble and rely on his strength, not our own human ability.

Part of our own insecurity can also come from blaming ourselves for what may have happened in the past. The wrong that we have done undermines any progress that we may make, because we do not put the past behind us and allow the fullness of God's forgiveness to take it away. The speaker in Job reminds us that if we reach out to God, putting the past – with its sin – away from us, then we can be secure in the hope that God gives to us as we follow him.

Spiritual activity

Think of the things which you feel most insecure doing: some may be quite trivial, others may have a significant effect on your life. Consider what God may be saying to you through that personal experience of life which is unique to you.

- Is he using those gifts and skills, strengths and weaknesses, as a signpost to where you should go and what you should do?

- Do we allow our weaknesses to act as a distraction, which then disables some of the progress and contribution we make in our faith?

Prayer

Lord, I look at my weaknesses, and sometimes I am fearful of being put in an embarrassing or vulnerable situation with which I cannot cope. Help me to focus my vision on the hope and strength that you give, in the knowledge that with you there is nothing that together we cannot overcome. I ask this for Jesus' sake. Amen.

THE TWENTY-EIGHTH DAY

Lack of faith

Bible readings

So they brought him. When the spirit saw Jesus, it immediately threw the boy into a convulsion. He fell to the ground and rolled around, foaming at the mouth. Jesus asked the boy's father, 'How long has he been like this?' 'From childhood,' he answered. 'It has often thrown him into fire or water to kill him. But if you can do anything, take pity on us and help us.' '"If you can"?' said Jesus. 'Everything is possible for him who believes.' Immediately the boy's father exclaimed, 'I do believe; help me overcome my unbelief!'

(Mark 9.20–24)

The apostles said to the Lord, 'Increase our faith!'

(Luke 17.5)

Now Thomas (called Didymus), one of the Twelve, was not with the disciples when Jesus came. When the other disciples told him that they had seen the Lord, he declared, 'Unless I see the nail marks in his hands and put my finger where the nails were, and put my hands into his side, I will not believe it.' A week later his disciples were in the house again, and Thomas was with them. Though the doors were locked, Jesus came and stood among them and said, 'Peace be with you!' Then he said to Thomas, 'Put your finger here; see my hands. Reach out your hand and put it into my side. Stop doubting and believe.' Thomas said to him, 'My Lord and my God!' Then Jesus told him, 'Because you have seen me, you have believed; blessed are those who have not seen and yet have believed.'

(John 20.24–29)

* * *

It is reassuring that the Bible contains several very human stories, where people are open and honest enough to express their lack of faith. It is significant that those stories are

83

actually told, because it shows us that having faith is not easy, that it can be a struggle and that Christ understands this. Those who are frank, and express the dilemmas they are in, are not condemned by Jesus, but rather are sympathetically encouraged by him. Those people he did condemn, however, were the ones who thought they had got their religious act together and had plenty of faith, and those who were just wilfully disobedient to the laws of God.

Therefore, if you are the first to admit that you lack faith then you are in the good position of being open and honest. Besides, even the apostles recognized that they needed more faith. It is, however, the spirit behind that honest confession that is important. A true recognition of what you lack should be a way to learn and discover more of what it means to have faith. While none of us should be complacent enough to think that we have adequate faith, we should be secure enough to be sure of the faith that has redeemed us, and made us children of God.

To recognize our lack of faith is an important opportunity because it expresses our willingness to grow, to learn and discover more. Failing to recognize it will mean we become distracted on our journey; we will find ourselves in a cul-de-sac, going nowhere. Admitting our lack of faith is to admit a powerful and fundamental truth for our lives; it is an opportunity for hope and growth. So do not see that honest admission in negative terms, it is actually supremely positive.

Do not bemoan your lack of faith, or use it as an excuse not to do anything, or deny that God has worked and can continue to work in you. Only the Devil will tell you, in a condemning way, that you do not have enough faith. He will say that you are no good, that you have not got enough of what it takes. Do not believe him – listening to him will do you no good. Rather, let your admission of lack of faith be a spring-board to help you move on, an opportunity to continue your God-given pilgrimage. Let it be a chance to celebrate all that you have discovered so far, and a hope of better things to come.

Spiritual activity

Identify the areas of faith where you are weak and where you know that you lack knowledge and understanding. This may simply be a matter of acknowledging the questions to which you need to seek answers. The next step is to identify where you can receive access to those answers. Does it involve some reading and study? If so, ask for the guidance of your clergy, or someone who exercises a role of spiritual leadership whom you know and respect. It may also involve you joining a particular study group.

Prayer

Lord, I recognize that I have a lot to learn, and that there are many areas of my life where my faith is weak. Give me a heart that is inspired to learn, so I may grow in faith and knowledge of you. Amen.

THE TWENTY-NINTH DAY

What will others say?

Bible readings

> How long must your servant wait?
> When will you punish my persecutors?
> The arrogant dig pitfalls for me, contrary to your law.
> All your commands are trustworthy;
> help me, for men persecute me without cause.
> They almost wiped me from the earth,
> but I have not forsaken your precepts.
> Preserve my life according to your love,
> and I will obey the statutes of your mouth.
>
> (Psalm 119.84–88)

> Blessed are you when people insult you, persecute you and falsely say all kinds of evil against you because of me. Rejoice and be glad, because great is your reward in heaven, for in the same way they persecuted the prophets who were before you.
>
> (Matthew 5.11–12)

> On that day a great persecution broke out against the church at Jerusalem, and all except the apostles were scattered throughout Judea and Samaria. Godly men buried Stephen and mourned deeply for him.
>
> (Acts 8.1–3)

* * *

Christianity was born out of the cradle of persecution. To come to Christ and confess your faith in him was no easy step; the consequences could lead to innumerable hardships – even death.

In the year AD 303, the Emperor Diocletian unleashed one of the most vicious persecutions against the faith. Churches were demolished, books were burnt and Christians were imprisoned, tortured and put to death. However, far from eradicating the Christian faith, the Church grew, as people witnessed the courage and sacrifice that many men and women made. For example, the story is told of 20 Christians who were sentenced to death by the Emperor. They were ordered to stand naked on a frozen lake overnight, where they would be out of sight of the public eye. Beside the lake was a small hut in which there was food and clothing, where they could freely go to if they renounced their faith. A guard was placed on duty by the hut. As the night wore on, the men gradually succumbed to the cold, until only two were still alive. One gave in under the pressure, and staggered off to the refuge of the shelter. However, the next morning, 20 bodies were found frozen to death on the lake. On examination, the Emperor was appalled to discover that one of the bodies was that of the centurion guard. The soldier had obviously been so moved by the courage of the 19 who remained faithful to their faith that he had taken the place of the one who had failed.

The early Church was the victim of the most irrational and abusive rumours; for example, that it carried out acts of ritual human sacrifice. The body and blood of Christ in the bread and wine were used in various propaganda campaigns against the Church to imply cannibalism. Persecution has continued in modern times as well: Christians have been persecuted under Communism, Fascism and various authoritarian dictatorships. For us, however, persecution may seem a far cry from the reality of our everyday Christian lives, where apathy and indifference are often the responses elicited in others. And yet even then we are afraid to stand up and identify with what we believe, for fear of upsetting someone. If the early Christians displayed as little courage as we sometimes exhibit, the Church would never have gone further than the borders of Palestine. So why do we spend so much time apologizing for our faith, and hoping that no one is offended? We do not want to deliberately offend any-one, yet by bending over backwards to make the faith socially acceptable we are in danger of presiding over a nation that has forgotten God, because of the deafening silence of the majority of Christians.

We can be distracted in our Christian pilgrimage by the simple anxiety of not wishing to upset anyone by our faith. It is easier to say very little, or not make a stand when we know that something is illegal or immoral. Yet Jesus says it is a blessed thing to suffer for his sake. For most of us that would not be likely to happen, since our hesitancy to say something for Christ usually dominates our thinking.

Fear of what others will say can obscure our calling and our journey of faith. That fear and hesitancy need to be overcome if we are to progress in our trust, and stand as a witness to God in a world that is confused, and does not know which way to turn.

Spiritual activity

- What have been some of the occasions recently when you could have made a stand for what you believe, but failed to do so?
- What have been the effects on you and those who you deal with, and their consequent results?
- How can you make a more faithful and clear witness to your Christian faith?

Prayer

Lord, forgive me for the times when I have not been a faithful witness for you. Help me to have courage, and not fear what others may think or say, recognizing that to suffer for you is an honour. Amen.

6

Anticipating our arrival

THE THIRTIETH DAY

Called by my name

Bible readings

O Lord, you have searched me and you know me.
You know when I sit and when I rise;
you perceive my thoughts from afar.
You discern my going out and my lying down;
you are familiar with all my ways.
Before a word is on my tongue
you know it completely, O Lord.

(Psalm 139.1–4)

Indeed, the very hairs of your head are all numbered.

(Luke 12.7a)

For this reason I kneel before the Father, from whom his whole
family in heaven and on earth derives its name. I pray that out
of his glorious riches he may strengthen you with power through
his Spirit in your inner being, so that Christ may dwell in your
hearts through faith. And I pray that you, being rooted and
established in love, may have power, together with all the saints,
to grasp how wide and long and high and deep is the love of
Christ, and to know this love that surpasses knowledge – that
you may be filled to the measure of all the fullness of God.

(Ephesians 3.14–19)

* * *

For a number of years I led a church youth group. They were a great bunch of teenagers; although totally exhausting to look after, they were a very exciting group of young people to be with. Each year, on Easter Monday, we used to go on a pilgrimage to Guildford Cathedral. We would begin walking at about 6.30 a.m. and would usually arrive in time for the youth service, which began at 3.00 p.m. It was the thought of that service, and the 2000 other pilgrims who would be there, that used to keep us going over the 20-mile trek.

As you approach Guildford, the Cathedral eventually looms into sight. It stands impressively on top of Stag Hill, looking down over the town, and once you see it you realize that you can begin to anticipate your arrival. But when on the pilgrimage, the journey is far from over. Visually, the Cathedral looks close as it dominates the landscape, but there are still the hills and inclines of the town to negotiate. The irony for us was that it was walking *down* the steep streets that was most painful on the leg muscles. What kept us going was the fact that the pilgrimage afforded the opportunity to talk and have a deeper sense of fellowship with those who were on the journey. On arrival at the Cathedral, it would be absolutely packed, and we usually had to find a place to sit on the floor somewhere. Despite being swallowed up in the crowd, we would be aware – painfully, as each muscle and limb ached! – that we, as individuals, had made the pilgrimage.

That awareness is always true. You and I may be one with millions and millions of God's children who, over the centuries, have passed through the pilgrimage of life, but we journey because we are called, and no one else can make our journey for us. What can continue to sustain us as we look ahead, anticipating our arrival, is the fact that God has called us out of his deep knowledge and love for us.

God knows us better than we know ourselves. There is nothing that is hidden from him. No thoughts, actions, plans or hopes are beyond God's knowing. Such is his intimate awareness of us as individuals, that even the number of hairs on our head are known to him. So although we journey alone, we are part of a great company of fellow pilgrims; more than that, we are secure in the knowledge of the one whose love for us is beyond the bounds of total comprehension.

Spiritual activity

Read Psalm 139.1–18. Spend a few minutes reflecting on what it says, then read it again, pausing after each verse.

Prayer

Father, I thank you that you know me, and have called me to follow you. All my life is under the gaze of your love, and held in the hands of your knowledge. Sustain me, I pray, until I come to the fullness of your presence, when all my days here on earth are done. Amen.

THE THIRTY-FIRST DAY

Listening to God

Bible readings

The Lord said, 'Go out and stand on the mountain in the presence of the Lord, for the Lord is about to pass by.' Then a great and powerful wind tore the mountain apart and shattered the rocks before the Lord, but the Lord was not in the wind. After the wind there was an earthquake, but the Lord was not in the earthquake. After the earthquake came a fire, but the Lord was not in the fire. And after the fire came a gentle whisper. When Elijah heard it, he pulled his cloak over his face and went out and stood at the mouth of the cave. Then a voice said to him, 'What are you doing here, Elijah?'

(1 Kings 19.11–13)

'I tell you the truth, the man who does not enter the sheep pen by the gate, but climbs in by some other way, is a thief and a robber. The man who enters by the gate is the shepherd of his sheep. The watchman opens the gate for him, and the sheep listen to his voice. He calls his own sheep by name and leads them out.'

(John 10.1–3)

'I am the good shepherd; I know my sheep and my sheep know me – just as the Father knows me and I know the Father – and I lay down my life for the sheep. I have other sheep who are not of this sheep pen. I must bring them also. They too will listen to my voice, and there shall be one flock and one shepherd.'

(John 10.14–16)

* * *

To some, the whole notion of listening to God is absurd because it presupposes that God speaks to us as individuals. Well, the fact is that he does. In the Old Testament, God speaks to various people because he wishes to communicate with them. A disciple is someone who is learning to listen to his or her

92

master's voice, someone who is discovering that the whole being – heart, mind, body and soul – can respond to God and listen to his calling. Elijah discovered the voice of God, not in the dramatic and the spectacular, but in the quiet and gentle. The New International Version of the Bible speaks of the gentle whisper, but the older versions use the memorable term, 'still small voice'.

As we progress in our personal pilgrimage, and learn and discover more of the reality of God's presence within us, so we are able to discern the voice of God, the voice of the shepherd who calls his sheep. But, in reality, what does this mean? How can we discern the real voice of God? The answer is that the voice of God speaks to us in a number of ways.

Firstly, and supremely, God speaks to us through the Bible. As we read the Bible, we need to listen to what it says and respond in obedience. We need to listen to God as he shows us how to live our lives, and the values that we should adopt as his children. If you ask God: 'What do you want me to do with my life?' you will find the answer through the guidance and advice in the Bible, which is inspired by God. Listen to it!

Secondly, the voice of God comes through the Holy Spirit, who prompts our thoughts and gives us the strong conviction that something is right or wrong. Since the Holy Spirit never contradicts the teachings of the Bible, you should know what the Bible says before you can be in tune with the prompting of the Holy Spirit. Or, at least, you must test the inner voice you hear, or the strong impression you are gaining, against the teaching of the Bible, so you can discern what is of God, and what are your own thoughts and ideas.

Thirdly, God's voice will come to us through common sense. God has given us minds to think with. He never intended that we should bypass our minds, and ignore all our human resources of thought and experience. As the Christian leader John Stott once said, 'God's promises of guidance were not given to save us the problem of thinking.'

Fourthly, no one is an island, certainly not in the Christian Church. I am very sceptical of a small minority of Christians who seem to have a personal hot line to God, so much so that they never seem to consult other Christians. Listening to God also means listening to others through whom God speaks. And, finally, we can listen to God by observing the situations that develop around us. If an opportunity comes about, it may well be God showing us the way forward. On the other hand, if circumstances deny certain options then we are possibly being guided in another direction.

To listen to God, therefore, is a matter of responding to the Bible, the Spirit, our mind, our fellow Christians and the circumstances around us. As we try to conform more and more to the will of God for our lives, so we will be better able and more experienced to listen to his voice.

Spiritual activity

Jesus said that the greatest and most important commandment was, 'You shall love the Lord your God with all your heart, with all your soul, with all your mind, and with all your strength'. Repeat these words to yourself up to 10 or 12 times and then reflect on what God is saying to you through them.

Prayer

Lord, speak to me and help me to listen. Help me to hear your voice among all the busyness and confusion of life. Help me to discern your ways and know your perfect will. Amen.

THE THIRTY-SECOND DAY

Ransomed

Bible readings

Then the people answered, 'Far be it from us to forsake the Lord to serve other gods! It was the Lord our God himself who brought us and our forefathers up out of Egypt, from that land of slavery, and performed those great signs before our eyes. He protected us on our entire journey and among all the nations through which we travelled. And the Lord drove out before us all the nations, including the Amorites, who lived in the land. We too will serve the Lord, because he is our God.'

(Joshua 24.16–18)

Jesus called them together and said, 'You know that the rulers of the Gentiles lord it over them, and their high officials exercise authority over them. Not so with you. Instead, whoever wants to become great among you must be your servant, and whoever wants to be first must be your slave – just as the Son of Man did not come to be served, but to serve, and give his life as a ransom for many.'

(Matthew 20.25–28)

This is good, and pleases God our Saviour, who wants all men to be saved and to come to a knowledge of the truth. For there is one God and one mediator between God and men, the man Christ Jesus, who gave himself as a ransom for all men – the testimony given in its proper time.

(1 Timothy 2.3–6)

* * *

'Ransomed' means the price paid for freedom. Who paid the price, however? Who was given the freedom? Well, the answer to the first question is clearly Christ. By his death on the Cross he paid the price for our sin. He took the responsibility for the guilt over all we have ever done wrong. Instead of taking the punishment ourselves, he became the substitute for us. There

95

was no one else who could perform the role of being the mediator between us and God.

As to the second question, *his* life was the ransom for *our* life. That life nailed to the Cross bought us freedom: freedom from the consequences and grip of sin; freedom to be as God intended us to be; freedom to serve God and others. As the theologian Hans Küng wrote, 'To be a Christian is to be truly human' (*On Being a Christian*, Fount Paperbacks, 1978). We are free to be the true people that God always intended us to be. Free – not to do what we want but what is right, what is good and what is true. We are called by God, and are able to listen to that calling, precisely because we have been ransomed. We are no longer condemned as guilty, accused by all that we have done wrong, but are forgiven because the price has been paid.

The tale is told of a young boy who used to go on holiday each year to the south coast with his parents. It was an event that they used to look forward to during the cold winter months. One year the boy decided to make a small boat in preparation for the forthcoming holiday. He put a great deal of time and effort into making his boat. He carefully carved the hull out of a block of wood, and used some of his mother's material to create the sails. He painted it and made it look as impressive as he could. When eventually the holiday time came he was extremely excited, anticipating whether all his hard work on the boat would be worthwhile. When they arrived at the hotel he rushed upstairs, hurriedly got changed, and persuaded his father to forgo the unpacking and go with him down to the beach. When they got there he carefully trimmed the sails and set his boat in the water. It worked! The boat sat stable in the water, looking proud and confident. So he gave it a gentle push and it gracefully moved in a circle, carried along by the gentle breeze. The young lad got a great deal of enjoyment out of sailing his boat, until on the third day disaster struck. The wind got up, and a sharp breeze suddenly altered the trim of the sail, affecting its course so much that it headed out to sea. No amount of effort by his father could rescue it, it just sailed out too far beyond his reach.

For days the boy searched along the beach hoping that the tide might have washed it ashore – but to no avail. The last day of the holiday dawned, and since the weather was wet the family decided to wander around the local shops. Walking past a junk shop, to their great surprise, they saw the boat sitting in the front window with a £2 price tag. Obviously, someone had found it and sold it to the shopkeeper. The boy was overjoyed and rushed back to the hotel, found the last of his holiday money and returned to the shop. He was jubilant as he left clutching his boat, and exclaimed, 'I made it and now I've bought it.'

That is exactly what God has done for us. He has made us, we are his creation, and he has bought us – it is Jesus who has paid the price.

Spiritual activity

Consider for a moment the parts of your life that are of greatest importance to you.

- What is the most precious item that you possess, or have responsibility for?
- What did it cost you to acquire that precious item?
- Was it money or was it something of greater value?
- If you lost it, what would you give for its safe return?

Prayer

Father, I thank you that in Christ you have ransomed me; that you have bought me with a price paid for in blood on the Cross. Having bought my freedom, help me to live as a free person, liberated from sin and guilt, and to rejoice in serving you. Amen.

THE THIRTY-THIRD DAY

Child of the Father

Bible readings

> He does not treat us as our sins deserve or repay us according
>   to our iniquities.
> For as high as the heavens are above the earth,
> so great is his love for those who fear him;
> as far as the east is from the west,
> so far has he removed our transgressions from us.
> As a father has compassion on his children,
> so the Lord has compassion on those who fear him.
>
> (Psalm 103.10–13)

> You are all sons of God through faith in Christ Jesus, for all
> of you who were baptized into Christ have clothed yourselves
> with Christ. There is neither Jew nor Greek, slave nor free, male
> nor female, for you are all one in Christ Jesus. If you belong to
> Christ, then you are Abraham's seed, and heirs according to his
> promise.
>
> (Galatians 3.26–29)

> He was in the world, and though the world was made through
> him, the world did not recognize him. He came to that which
> was his own, but his own did not receive him. Yet to all who
> received him, to those who believed in his name, he gave the
> right to become children of God – children born not of natural
> descent, nor of human decision or a husband's will, but born
> of God.
>
> (John 1.10–13)

* * *

Sometimes we seem to remember the strangest things from childhood days; events that our own parents may have forgotten,
for example, but which have made such an impression on us
that we have never forgotten them. I remember that whenever
I was unwell, my father would always hold my head gently in

98

his hand as I peered down the toilet being ill. He would then put me back to bed, and stroke my hair until I fell asleep. As a child, it is always reassuring to have Mum or Dad present at that most undesirable moment when you are physically being ill. To be comforted afterwards always makes the discomfort much more bearable.

One evening, some years ago, when our elder son Alastair was two years old and could not get to sleep, we were not sure what was wrong, since he really could not tell us if anything hurt. He was getting quite distressed, as he kept on waking up every 45 minutes or so. As I cuddled him and tried to calm him down, I remembered what my father had done, and so when I put him back in bed, I gently stroked his hair. The effect was the same as it had been on me, and he relaxed and went back to sleep.

I am lucky because I have had parents whom I love and admire; sadly, that is not true for everyone. What is wonderful is that we all have a heavenly Father who does not have the imperfections of earthly parents. His love is pure and perfect and has no bounds. Until we see God face to face, we will never fully understand how much he loves us. We may never have conceived the times he has wept over us, and tried to guide us in the right paths; the times he has spoken to us, yet we have not listened or heeded his calling. Yet if we fear him – in other words, respect him – and give him the honour that is right-fully his, he is compassionate towards us.

Children who are deliberately disobedient create an environ-ment of conflict that is difficult to manage. But when a child is being co-operative, possibly even getting things wrong, then a parent's attitude is far more understanding. So it is with God. If we are trying to follow him, despite having made (and continuing to make) mistakes, then God is there trying to see us through. But if there is no basic respect or attempt at obedience to God, then the barriers to a positive and creative relationship are raised higher.

To be a child of the Heavenly Father is a great joy and a total privilege. In fact, no one on earth could bestow on you a greater honour. The New Year's Honours List, and the worthy rewards it bestows, pales into insignificance against the distinction of knowing you are an heir to the promises of God! You have an inheritance that is kept in heaven, which no one can take from you, and which even now transforms your present reality.

Spiritual activity

- Looking at your own children – or, if you do not have children of your own, at the offspring of friends – what do you enjoy doing with them? Playing football? Craft activities? Talking with them? Getting them to share their thoughts and feelings with you?
- What are the special aspects of a child–parent relationship, and what do they tell us about the nature of our potential and actual relationship with our Heavenly Father?

Prayer

Father, I cannot pretend that I fully fathom all of your love. I cannot pretend that I recognize, or totally appreciate, the reality of what you have done for me. But I thank you for the privilege of being your child. Help me to live out and express the reality of that truth in my life today. Amen.

THE THIRTY-FOURTH DAY

Knowing

Bible readings

I will take you as my own people, and I will be your God. Then you will know that I am the Lord your God, who brought you out from under the yoke of the Egyptians.

(Exodus 6.7)

'Be still, and know that I am God;
I will be exalted among the nations,
I will be exalted in the earth.'

(Psalm 46.10)

We know also that the Son of God has come and has given us understanding, so that we may know him who is true. And we are in him who is true – even in his Son Jesus Christ. He is the true God and eternal life.

(1 John 5.20)

After Jesus said this, he looked towards heaven and prayed: 'Father, the time has come. Glorify your Son, that your Son may glorify you. For you have granted him authority over all people that he might give eternal life to all those you have given him. Now this is eternal life: that they may know you, the only true God, and Jesus Christ, whom you have sent. I have brought you glory on earth by completing the work you gave me to do. And now, Father, glorify me in your presence with the glory I had with you before the world began.'

(John 17.1–5)

* * *

The word 'know' occurs a staggering number of times in the Bible, and in a variety of ways – one of which is the phrase, 'know that I am the Lord'. Another phrase is concerned with the 'knowledge of God'. All this reveals a simply breathtaking truth that God can be known! The power of that reality is awesome.

101

Each one of us can know a lot of things in life, and in a real sense knowledge is power. But some of our knowledge may be to do with those areas that are only relevant to ourselves, and which may not be of any greater significance, whereas other forms of knowledge are matters of life and death. To know where the brakes are in the car, for example, might be rather important when it comes to being a safe driver, and living a long and happy life.

The knowledge that is spoken about in the Bible, however, means knowledge of our personal relationship with God. The simple truth is that God can be known. There is no one else in life and death whom it is more important to know. He can be known at a personal level so that we have a relationship with him that is built on love, trust and experience. To not know God is the greatest tragedy of life. But to know him, and as a pilgrim to grow in that knowledge, is the most satisfying and joyful relationship in life, which even overcomes death.

The biggest challenge to us as Christian people is to grow in that knowledge of God. I am very fortunate to have many dear friends, whose love and companionship I have enjoyed immensely over the years. I am sure the same is true for you. When I think about those friendships, the reason why they run so deep is that we have made the effort to spend time with each other. After moving to a new town some years ago, and meeting a lot of new people, I initially wondered why I did not seem to have the same rapport with our new friends. At first, I was rather anxious about this. Then I realized that we had known all our other friends for several years and had shared a lot with them. There is no substitute for time; deep relationships take time. It takes time to build up a high degree of trust in and knowledge of someone else.

In the same way, it takes time to grow and be sensitive in our knowledge of the living God. We need to spend time and make a real effort to get to know God. Developing that friendship will be the most valuable and the most meaningful relationship of our entire lives. It is therefore worth making sacrifices, in terms of time and energy, to focus on the most important relationship we can ever experience.

Spiritual activity

Think of the special relationships that you have which make up your life.

- What is it that makes those relationships so valuable?
- What can you identify from them that would develop and strengthen your relationship with God?

Prayer

Lord, I thank you for the joy and privilege of knowing you. My relationship with you is the most important thing in my life. Help me to renew and deepen those bonds of friendship, until the day that I will see you face to face. Amen.

THE THIRTY-FIFTH DAY

Experiencing love

Bible readings

He who dwells in the shelter of the Most High
will rest in the shadow of the Almighty.
I will say of the Lord, 'He is my refuge and my fortress,
    my God, in whom I trust.'
'Because he loves me,' says the Lord, 'I will rescue him;
I will protect him, for he acknowledges my name.
He will call upon me, and I will answer him;
I will be with him in trouble,
I will deliver him and honour him.
With long life will I satisfy him
and show him my salvation.'

(Psalm 91.1–2, 14–16)

Therefore, since we have been justified through faith, we have
peace with God through our Lord Jesus Christ, through whom
we have gained access by faith into this grace in which we now
stand. And we rejoice in the hope of the glory of God. Not only
so, but we also rejoice in our sufferings, because we know that
suffering produces perseverance; perseverance, character; and
character, hope. And hope does not disappoint us, because God
has poured out his love into our hearts by the Holy Spirit, whom
he has given us.

(Romans 5.1–5)

This is love: not that we loved God, but that he loved us and
sent his Son as an atoning sacrifice for our sins. Dear friends,
since God so loved us, we also ought to love one another. No
one has ever seen God; but if we love one another, God lives in
us and his love is made complete in us.

(1 John 4.10–12)

* * *

The joy of the Christian faith comes from the reality of experiencing God's love. It is a love that one can know intellectually, emotionally and spiritually. After all, we are commanded to love God with all our heart, mind and strength. What we are asked to give back is only a shadow of what is on offer to us. The joy that is released within us, and the peace of God, comes from experiencing that divine love. When we realize that, he becomes our refuge and shelter, the one we can trust throughout life with all its mess and confusion, the one we can turn to because he offers salvation and security born out of an eternal and ever present love.

We begin to experience the full force of God's love when we accept that it is not what *we* can do that is essential, but rather what God has already done; not that we love God but that he loves us. That is when we begin to celebrate and know the divine love. In your prayers and celebration you can get lost in the love, moved to tears in that love, and transformed in that love. If you have never said to God 'I love you', you may not have heard him saying it to you. This love is personal, it is real, and it is offered to you and me. It is to be enjoyed, experienced, known and celebrated.

I proposed to my wife, late one night, on Waterloo Bridge. I knew that it was one of her favourite places in London because you can see so many attractive locations along the River Thames.

For both of us emotions were running pretty high, both leading up to the proposal and for a long time after her acceptance. When you realize that someone else loves you for who and what you are, it is an immensely powerful experience – in some circumstances it can be life changing. It is the same with God's offer of love to us – it has to be accepted and responded to if we are to experience its reality. The Christian faith, like marriage, has its emotional highs and lows; our feelings will change, but the reality remains the same. That love is for keeps.

Spiritual activity

Scribble down a few notes about what you felt when your spouse or closest friend expressed their love for you. You may wish to write sentences or just put down some key words. Then write down what you felt when it began to dawn on you that God loves you. What are the similarities in what you felt and experienced?

Prayer

Lord, I love you, but most of all thank you for loving me.
Amen.

7

Coming home

————◆•◆◆————

THE THIRTY-SIXTH DAY

Alone and secure

Bible readings

> The Lord is good to those whose hope is in him, to the one who
> seeks him; it is good to wait quietly for the salvation of the Lord.
> It is good for a man to bear the yoke while he is young. Let him
> sit alone in silence, for the Lord has laid it on him.
>
> (Lamentations 3.25–28)

> You will be secure, because there is hope; you will look about
> you and take your rest in safety. You will lie down, with no one
> to make you afraid, and many will court your favour.
>
> (Job 11.18–19)

> After the people saw the miraculous sign that Jesus did, they
> began to say, 'Surely this is the Prophet who is to come into the
> world.' Jesus, knowing that they intended to come and make
> him king by force, withdrew again to a mountain by himself.
>
> (John 6.14–15)

* * *

Your spiritual journey is yours and yours alone. No one can
tread that path for you. No one on earth can be your substitute.
The path you walk is the path given to you by God himself,
marked out in your own personal destiny.

Do not be afraid to be alone, because in the solitude you will discover more about yourself, and come to know more of the one who calls you. When the distractions of the crowd were attempting to divert Jesus, what did he do but withdraw to be alone! Like Jesus, we can experience the worldly powers of distraction all around us, which may appear well intentioned, yet do not fully understand us and the path we are called to follow. It is then that we need to stand back, and to see ourselves and our situation as God sees them, not as others want them to be. We should be like the Prodigal Son, who needed to recognize his personal circumstances and make his own journey home. In many ways, our own feelings of being alone are heightened as we draw closer to our destination. We experience the sense of having come a long way, that now it is us alone who stand on the threshold of embracing that which we have been approaching. But that sense of ourselves should not make us afraid. Indeed, the most profound spiritual experiences are often to be found in silence, and being alone with God – our ultimate security.

One of the present dangers in the Church is that individuals are seeking yet more spiritual experiences and blessings. It seems that we have become victims of spiritual consumerism, in that the latest brand of experience is better or more powerful than the last. It is difficult to anticipate where it will all end, but there will be many empty and dissatisfied souls, unless we see that silence – and being alone with God – is at the centre of our calling. The nature of faith is a relationship built on the security of Father and child. Spiritual experiences, as valuable and desirable as they may be, are not central to the core relationship. If we put experiences before that personal and individual relationship, we will have a very insecure faith. Be patient and seek God for himself, because he has called you as his disciple.

Spiritual activity

Take at least five minutes out of your day to escape from all the demands of friends and work, and to be by yourself. Retreat to somewhere where you can be alone in your thoughts and prayers. Take the opportunity to listen to yourself and to God. Do not try to find an answer or a message or understand – just listen.

Prayer

Lord, in quietness and solitude you are my refuge and my strength, and underneath are your everlasting arms, holding me secure. Amen.

THE THIRTY-SEVENTH DAY

Purpose fulfilled

Bible readings

All this took place to fulfil what the Lord had said through the prophet: 'The virgin will be with child and will give birth to a son, and they will call him Immanuel' – which means, 'God with us'.

(Matthew 1.22–23)

Now there was a man in Jerusalem called Simeon, who was righteous and devout. He was waiting for the consolation of Israel, and the Holy Spirit was upon him. It had been revealed to him by the Holy Spirit that he would not die before he had seen the Lord's Christ. Moved by the Spirit, he went into the temple courts. When the parents brought the child Jesus to do for him what the custom of the Law required, Simeon took him in his arms and praised God, saying:

'Sovereign Lord, as you have promised, you now dismiss your servant in peace. For my eyes have seen your salvation, which you have prepared in the sight of all people, a light for revelation to the Gentiles and for glory to your people Israel.'

(Luke 2.25–32)

* * *

I always find the story of Simeon very moving and heart-warming. He is only mentioned in Luke's Gospel, and breaks into the story simply because he witnesses to Jesus, the promised one sent from God. Simeon was a patient man, who longed to see the ways of God come to the people of Israel. I am sure he must have been a very attractive, interesting person from whom one could have learnt a great deal. The passage describes him as righteous and devout, and that the Holy Spirit was upon him. I think this was the key to the fulfilment that he experienced.

110

His lifestyle expressed the things in life that were good and holy; his faith was translated into action, and expressed itself in his attitudes and values.

His trust in God was at the centre of his reason for living, and would have affected the way he looked at life, and the way he handled other people. Simeon's righteousness came from God and it was to God he expressed his gratitude in corporate worship and private prayer. He was obviously a man who listened to God and responded to him, hence the reason that the Holy Spirit was upon him. It is worth bearing in mind that Luke firstly says that he was righteous and devout, before going on to mention the Holy Spirit. This reminds us that there are no short cuts to being filled with the Spirit. Doing what God wants and living our lives in faithful obedience to him come first as an act of will and obedience. Only then is God able to fill us with his Spirit.

Through the Spirit, Simeon is aware that he is privileged to witness (before he dies) the coming of the one who is to be the fulfilment of Israel's – indeed, the world's – hope, the Messiah promised by God. It must have been a very moving and touching moment when he held Christ in his arms, for the words that he uttered betray a real power and beauty.

I consider Simeon to be a strong model for us to reflect on, and a source of real hope. We are called, like him, to be righteous, and to put into action the principles and ways of God into our daily lives. We are called to be devout, not in a falsely religious sense, but in a way that comes from the heart. A genuine love and gratitude to God our Saviour is required; we are called to be filled with God's Holy Spirit – the Spirit that makes the truth of God real in our lives, so that we can accomplish what God wants us to do. This is where we find true fulfilment.

Simeon was privileged to see the coming of the Messiah, but we can equally know the growing reality of Christ in our lives, the reality that satisfies us in a way nothing else can. We can find spiritual fulfilment through the divine purpose that bridges this life and the next. The benefits and privileges of being a pilgrim people are that we are on a path that is moving on up to being enfolded in the overwhelming eternal love of God.

Spiritual activity

Very often, those things that fulfil us are not immediate, but come out of a long-term commitment. Think for a few moments about some of the key aspects of your life that give you a deep sense of satisfaction and fulfilment, and the reasons behind them. Reflect on the spiritual lessons behind your feelings, and what you can learn about your own Christian commitment as a result.

Prayer

Father, thank you for the fulfilment that can be found in following your ways, and the depth of satisfaction from knowing the reality of your endless love. Amen.

THE THIRTY-EIGHTH DAY

Deliverance and freedom

Bible readings

Hide your face from my sins and blot out all my iniquity.
Create in me a pure heart, O God,
and renew a steadfast spirit within me.
Do not cast me from your presence
or take your Holy Spirit from me.
Restore to me the joy of your salvation
and grant me a willing spirit, to sustain me.

(Psalm 51.9–12)

'The Spirit of the Lord is on me, because he has anointed me
to preach good news to the poor. He has sent me to proclaim
freedom for the prisoners and recovery of sight for the blind,
to release the oppressed, to proclaim the year of the Lord's
favour.'

(Luke 4.18–19)

To the Jews who had believed in him, Jesus said, 'If you hold to
my teaching, you are really my disciples. Then you will know
the truth, and the truth will set you free.'

(John 8.32)

It is for freedom that Christ has set us free. Stand firm, then,
and do not let yourselves be burdened again by a yoke of
slavery.

(Galatians 5.1)

* * *

Deliverance and freedom are part of the rich heritage that is
ours as Christians. We celebrate that reality because it is all part
of what Christ has won for us. Any homecoming will have that
dimension as part of the joy that we experience.

The deliverance that has been won for us takes on many
different facets, and at a personal level we probably can testify

to some attitudes, or behaviour, that God has delivered us from as we have submitted our lives to him. The core of what God has done revolves around the fact that he has delivered us from sin, and all its accompanying guilt. While we still may have to live with the consequences of that sin, in terms of broken relationships, sexual disasters, financial irregularities and so on, ultimately the final result of all that we have done wrong is that our punishment has been accepted by Jesus. And if that is not good news, what is?

What Jesus offers has many different facets. For example, he offers good news for the poor. Who are the poor – those who are not materially well off? Or those who have everything but have nothing, who are chasing the empty satisfaction of materialism? Christ offers them deliverance to a better way, a way that offers hope of fulfilment at a much deeper level.

He also proclaims freedom to the prisoner. Does that just refer to those locked up in jail, or does it also mean freedom to those restricted by destructive habits and depersonalized relationships that set no value on people in their own right? He says he will make the blind see again. Does he mean he will restore the vision of those who are blind, or is he speaking about a whole new way of seeing life, values, people, purpose and meaning?

He speaks about bringing release to the oppressed. Is he just making a political statement about human rights abuses, or is he speaking about the oppression of all that denies our human worth such as drug abuse, sexual promiscuity and materialism? One writer, Arthur Radford, hit the nail on the head when he said, 'In the Bible, and particularly in Jesus' spiritual concepts of God and man, all men can find the key to victory, not only over one evil system, but in the greater crusade against all falsehood. Mankind, however, appears to come slowly to the realization that Freedom is not won and held solely by material means.'

Jesus' deliverance is about the fundamental freedom that can be experienced at every level, because it is about truth and reality. It is the truth that sees everything in real perspective. It is about the light that overcomes the darkness which obscures and hides what is authentic.

As we make our journey home we are called to live in this freedom, and to know the full truth of it. The result will be that our lives will resonate with what is genuine, beautiful, of meaning and substance, and after the likeness of God himself.

Spiritual activity

- If you were not a follower of Jesus Christ, what spiritual, and moral values would you be living your life by at this moment in time?
- Would you be in a different job or on a different income?
- Would your relationships be based on different values?
- Would you have a different husband or wife, or boyfriend or girlfriend?
- What has Christ set you free from, and how has he caused you to travel in a different direction?

Prayer

Lord, thank you for the deliverance you have won for me on the Cross. Help my life to reflect the freedom you have purchased for me in my values, and my lifestyle. Amen.

THE THIRTY-NINTH DAY

Secure in believing

Bible readings

'Listen to me, O house of Jacob, all you who remain of the house of Israel, you whom I have upheld since you were conceived, and have carried since your birth. Even to your old age and grey hairs I am he, I am he who will sustain you. I have made you and I will carry you; I will sustain you and I will rescue you.'

(Isaiah 46.3–4)

Now to him who is able to do immeasurably more than all we ask or imagine, according to his power that is at work within us, to him be glory in the church and in Christ Jesus throughout all generations, for ever and ever! Amen.

(Ephesians 3.20–21)

'Do not let your hearts be troubled. Trust in God; trust also in me. In my Father's house are many rooms; if it were not so, I would have told you. I am going there to prepare a place for you. And if I go and prepare a place for you, I will come back and take you to be with me that you also may be where I am. You know the way to the place where I am going.' Thomas said to him, 'Lord, we don't know where you are going, so how can we know the way?' Jesus answered. 'I am the way and the truth and the life. No-one comes to the Father except through me.'

(John 14.1–6)

* * *

Since we live in a society where, unfortunately, the security of our goods is not very certain, a huge industry of house and car alarms has developed to try to deter a thief from breaking in and stealing our possessions. Once, my own parents were burgled, and many valuable items were taken. I witnessed at first hand the traumatic effect that it had on them – it took months to come to terms with, being a very unpleasant experience.

Rightly, we are concerned about the security of our goods, but we must also consider our own personal sense of security. Here, however, we cannot necessarily influence our personal circumstances. If you are fortunate to come from a loving family background, then that can be an immense help in terms of what you feel about yourself. Conversely, I recently went to visit a mother who wanted her two children to be baptized. The baby was three months old, and the toddler just over two years old. Her husband deserted them when the baby was born, and left her to bring up the children alone. I could not help feeling sorry for all of them because of the insecurity of their future, and the effect that loss would have – especially on the children.

Our own personal sense of security fundamentally influences our developing personality. It is here that the Christian path potentially can be a huge influence, because we are offered the ultimate security: believing in God. It is in him that we find our true home; he is the sustainer of our very existence. What we see in the beautiful passage from Isaiah is that God has been with us from the point of our conception, and he will continue to be there right to the end. Even if our human circumstances may not have been the best, the power that is at work within us is greater than we can ever conceive or imagine. Moreover, while God can offer us security in himself for this life, he offers it for the next life as well. In fact, he has already gone to prepare a place for us.

Believing and trusting in God can create and develop in us – his children – the greatest sense of security which affects the way we feel about ourselves and changes the way we relate to those around us. Do we need to be frightened that others will not accept us when God accepts us? Do we need to be the centre of attention when we already have God's love and attention? We need not feel insecure about ourselves because we believe in the one who believes in us.

Spiritual activity

What are the situations which make you feel insecure? Are they circumstances at work, or particular relationships, for example? Think about these feelings that make you feel vulnerable and uncertain. Then consider them in the light of the truth of God's care for you. How can that help change what you feel about yourself and others?

Prayer

Lord, I thank you that you have sustained me from the very first moment, even though I did not have an awareness of you. Help me to commit to you my past, my present and all my future. Help me to see that you hold me in your arms, and that I am secure in your love. Amen.

THE FORTIETH DAY

Hope upheld

Bible readings

So do not fear, for I am with you; do not be dismayed, for I am your God. I will strengthen you and help you; I will uphold you with my righteous hand.

(Isaiah 41.10)

However, as it is written: 'No eye has seen, no ear has heard, no mind has conceived what God has prepared for those who love him.'

(1 Corinthians 2.9)

No-one has ever gone into heaven except the one who came from heaven – the Son of Man. Just as Moses lifted up the snake in the desert, so the Son of Man must be lifted up, that everyone who believes in him may have eternal life. For God so loved the world that he gave his one and only Son, that whoever believes in him shall not perish but have eternal life. For God did not send his Son into the world to condemn the world, but to save the world through him.

(John 3.13–17)

'My sheep listen to my voice; I know them, and they follow me. I give them eternal life, and they shall never perish; no-one can snatch them out of my hand. My Father, who has given them to me, is greater than all; no one can snatch them out of my Father's hand. I and the Father are one.'

(John 10.27–30)

* * *

When you approach home you are on the final part of your journey. You can see where you are going, and you have a glimpse of what you will find when you get there. So it is with us, a pilgrim people, as we move on up to the wonderful promise that is ours in Jesus. Because we follow him, no one can take away the hope and inheritance that is ours, held in trust for us by God himself. God is right there with us, encouraging us all the way. This is what makes the Christian life so exciting and worthwhile. Not only is it the right way to go but, with God calling and guiding us, we are upheld by his continual mercy and surrounding love.

Although we do not deserve all the love that God shows to us, he shares it with us out of the goodness of his heart. I have often been angry with God, resentful of the pain and anguish of what I have had to go through. I have often shouted at him: 'Why? Why? Why?' But I have always known that I was his, and that he knew and understood what I felt. When I wanted to rebel against him out of a resentment of how events were working out, I somehow felt that I would be hurting him and ultimately myself if I did so. But God kept me safe and upheld me with his right hand when I had had enough, and could not go on any longer.

We celebrate God who cherishes and loves us. Thank you for journeying with me as we have travelled along the way, through the wonderful Bible passages that God has given to us. I pray, as we continue that journey, that all of us will grow in our knowledge and understanding of the reality of the Living Christ, who is Lord of life and death.

Spiritual activity

What have you discovered or relearnt as you have been reading this book? If you get the chance, jot down some points. Take time to think about those areas which are very personal to you. How are you going to build and develop those lessons in your own lifestyle and Christian discipleship?

Prayer

Lord, I thank you for the wonder of your eternal love: a love that is so powerful that even death cannot divide us from you;

a love that is so personal it causes you to walk with us day by day. Help me to be sustained and empowered by your love for the rest of my life. I ask this in the name of the one who lived and died for us, my Saviour, Jesus Christ. Amen.

8

House group discussion and activity material

On the first occasion you meet, start by sharing a meal together. Eating together helps to break the ice and produces a positive and relaxed atmosphere. You either can have a 'bring and share' meal, where each member brings something savoury or sweet to share with others, or you could simply have dessert and coffee. Alternatively, you could eat together every evening the house group meets, if it does not put too much pressure on the host.

As the house group leader, it is important to remember that when using any questions or material always adapt them as necessary to suit your group. Add some material of your own if you wish, and use the sections in the book on spiritual activity to reinforce the points being discussed.

Session 1: Where are we going?

Discussion questions

(All the discussion questions make the assumption that each member has read the daily sections of the book.)

- Can members of the group identify any personal things they have had to leave behind in making their Christian pilgrimage?
- Where do we see the compassionate nature of God expressing itself in life? Give some concrete examples, both biblical and contemporary.

- Can any members of the group express what the grace of God means to them?
- Read again the three Bible passages from the third day and discuss the implications of what they are saying.
- Have there been times when your lives have been particularly difficult? How have you come through that experience?
- What examples of faithfulness to the cause of justice and faith can you give?
- Is it easy to forgive?
- What has this section taught us about the nature of God and how is that relevant to our daily lives?

Activity

Give each member a large piece of paper and a coloured pen, and instruct them to put a mark on the bottom right-hand corner to represent the day he or she was born, and a mark on the top left-hand corner to represent the present day. Then, ask everyone to draw a map of their life, beginning at their birth, pictorially indicating any significant events along the way. For example, a stay in hospital, their first school, places they have lived, jobs they have done. Then, according to the size of the group, either get each person to explain to everyone what they have drawn or, if there are a lot of people in the group, divide them up into pairs to discuss it. The benefit of this activity is that by first drawing on paper some of the significant events of their life, many people find it easier to talk to others about it. The effect is to deepen the fellowship and understanding of the group.

Session 2: Excess baggage

Discussion questions
- Why do we find someone crying difficult to handle?
- What are the positive aspects of tears?
- If you were given the chance to change one thing from the past what would you choose to alter?

- What have been some of the valuable lessons you have learnt from your failures in life?
- Read again the Bible passages from the ninth day and discuss the message that they have for us.
- How difficult is it to get an honest appraisal of ourselves?

Activity

Give everyone a blank piece of A4 paper and ask them to write their name at the top and then fold the paper in half. The group should then stand and circulate around the room. Hand over the paper and ask each person in turn to write something positive about the relevant person. Take care not to show the paper to the person to whom it belongs; they must not look at it when it is being circulated. When this has been done and each paper has been returned to its owner let them look at their sheet. Ask each person to identify one good thing that has been written down and to share it with the group. How might they improve on that good comment?

Session 3: Essentials for the journey

Discussion questions

- What are the implications of being 'In Christ', as St Paul describes the Christian life?
- What were your reactions when you read the story in the thirteenth day about the young boy and his mother?
- What parts of Jesus' teachings do you find difficult and unreasonable?
- How would you describe the friendship that Jesus offers to us?
- How would you explain this description to an inquirer?
- Can you recall and recount the time when you became aware that God was calling you to follow him?

Activity

Ask each person in turn to recount something positive that has happened since the group last met. Then ask whether there is anything that people would like others to remember in prayer until you meet again.

Session 4: Fit for the road

Discussion questions

- How have you seen the Holy Spirit work in your lives?
- Read again the three passages in the eighteenth day and discuss the significance of what they are saying.
- Over the past six months, what new aspects have you discovered about the Christian faith?
- Have there been recent examples in your church that have caused controversy because they have involved change? What about in the Church nationally? What do you think would be God's attitude to the argument?
- Look at Romans 12.1–2 in the twenty-first day. What did St Paul mean by offering your bodies as living sacrifices and being transformed by the renewing of your minds?
- Have there been times in your lives when you have been particularly aware of the power of God – either in the ability to do a task or simply the sense of God's presence?

Activity

At the end of the session place a lighted candle in the centre of the group. Turn off the lights and sit quietly for a few minutes concentrating on the beauty of the candle. Then invite people to say some very simple prayers – maybe no more than one sentence – thanking God for whatever they feel is appropriate. Close by joining hands and saying the Grace together.

Session 5: Distractions on the way

Discussion questions

- What sort of excuses do people today use to get out of following God?
- Do any of Moses' excuses to God in the biblical references in the twenty-fourth day sound familiar to you?
- What aspect of God frightens and causes you a sense of anxiety?
- If there was one request that you would least like God to put to you and to do what would it be?
- How can we help and encourage those members of our church and parish who are struggling with life and who find the Christian path a hard road to follow?
- What sort of security do you find your Christian faith gives you?
- What areas of faith would your house group like to explore when organizing another cause?
- Can you give examples of any negative reactions that you have had from people when you have tried to share your faith?
- Alternatively, have you ever received positive support when you least expected it?

Activity

Give everyone a pen and a large sheet of paper. Ask them to draw two lines which divide the paper into quarters. Then ask them to draw in each quarter something that has been uppermost in their thoughts over the past week. When they have completed their drawings, either divide them into pairs or into fours to explain their pictures, or let each person share what they have drawn with the whole group.

Session 6: Anticipating our arrival

Discussion questions

- How have you experienced what you understand to be the voice of God?
- How did this happen?
- Have you ever gone to considerable efforts to assist someone, only for him or her to be very ungrateful for all your troubles?
- What parallels can you see through that experience with the efforts and price that Jesus paid to ransom us?

Look at the three passages in the thirty-second day and discuss their meaning and implication for our lives.

- In what sense can we know God for ourselves? Discuss and unpack the meaning of the word 'know' as it is used in the Bible.
- In what ways should the Church be a channel for God's love? In what ways should it not be?

Activity

Ask members of the group to describe their first reactions to the neighbourhood when they first arrived and settled down.

Session 7: Coming home

Discussion questions

- As a house group and a church, and at an individual and corporate level, do you find silence a difficult situation to deal with?
- Are you discovering the power and value of silence?
- How can we live out a genuine righteousness and devotion to God today?
- What stops us from doing that?

- What sense of freedom do you feel is most relevant in your Christian life at the present moment?
- Can you identify those areas which make us feel insecure and contrast them with those that deepen a sense of genuine security in our lives?
- If you were asked to describe heaven, what words would you use to try and apprehend something of what it may be like?
- Have you already discovered something of what heaven may be like?

Activity

Ask your priest or minister to celebrate Communion for you as a group, as an act of fellowship together and as a climax to the experience of what you have shared together in reading *The Journey Home.*